# LORENZO AMORUSO

## THE OFFICIAL AUTOBIOGRAPHY

## L.A. CONFIDENTIAL

## David McCarthy
## and Keith Jackson

# LORENZO AMORUSO
# L.A. CONFIDENTIAL

Published by the Daily Record, One Central Quay, Glasgow, G38 DA.
Copyright: The Daily Record

Cover Picture: Alan Peebles

Edited and designed by First Press Publishing,
One Central Quay, Glasgow, G38DA.

ISBN 0-9513471-8-7

Printed and bound in Scotland

FIRST PRESS
PUBLISHING
DAILY RECORD AND SUNDAY MAIL MAGAZINE DIVISION

*I dedicate this book to my family, especially to my mother Antonietta and father Mauro. They made me the man I am today and I owe them everything.*

*There are not enough pages in this book for me to name and thank everyone who has touched my life and helped me on the journey to where I am today.*

*I apologise to them for that but they know who they are already. Let's just say they are the people who know the real Lorenzo.*

*Also, I would like to say a special word for a very dear friend of mine who passed away back home in Florence a month ago.*

*Don Giancarlo Setti was a priest and a fine human being who helped me through some of the darkest days of my life. He was a wonderful man who I could talk to about anything. I miss him and I thank him.*

**Lorenzo Amoruso**

# CONTENTS

# Chapter One

## ADVOCAAT AND THE ARMBAND

I REMEMBER the date as if it were yesterday. Monday, October 30, 2000… the day Dick Advocaat tried to rip my heart out.

It started like any other day. It ended with my life turned upside down and with me wanting to walk away from the club I had grown to love.

Being given the captaincy of Rangers was one of the biggest honours ever bestowed upon me and now the man who had made the decision to do that – and had been repaid by me leading this great team to five trophies out of six over the two previous seasons – was sitting in his office at the top of the marble staircase at Ibrox telling me that I was no longer to be captain of this great club.

We'd lost three games in a row in the league, 1-0 against Hibs at Easter Road and 2-1 away to St Johnstone before a 3-0 defeat against Kilmarnock at Ibrox. We had also only drawn at home to Galatasaray in the Champions League and lost 2-0 to Sturm Graz to leave us struggling to make the next round.

A club like Rangers is almost unique because if it loses even two games in a row the fans are going mad and the newspapers are full of crisis headlines. So you can imagine how people were feeling about us losing four out of five and only drawing the other one.

The fans were unhappy. Okay, it was worse than that – they were going crazy – and the dressing room was depressed. But it was also divided and that showed in the way we were performing on the park.

The game against Kilmarnock was a really bad one. We deservedly lost 3-0 in front of our own fans and everybody played badly. No exceptions.

We were in complete disarray at that point in the season. Already Celtic had a lead on us at the top of the table and we needed to become more focused, more determined.

On the Monday after that defeat I left the dressing room to find the manager because the boys were struggling to understand a certain system he was trying to get us to play. We were getting mixed up and it was showing on the park.

As captain it was my responsibility to speak on behalf of the players, so I went to let him know there was a bit of confusion and to ask him if he would come and explain exactly what he wanted us to do.

Advocaat listened to me but his face was impassive – he would make a brilliant poker player because his expression very rarely changed. Then he opened his mouth and when the words came out I honestly thought something had short-circuited in my brain and that I was hearing different words from what he was actually saying.

Within seconds I realised there was nothing wrong with me. This man really was telling me that I was no longer captain of Rangers.

He said: "Some players are unhappy with the way you are behaving in the dressing room, so I am changing the captaincy."

I am a very strong character and if we lose, or if the team plays badly, then I am not afraid to voice my opinion and shout in the dressing room at the end of a game.

I don't apologise for that. Every player should be angry if he loses a match. We all know it can happen sometimes but if the team has not given everything then people should be angry and upset – and I was.

I was telling them that we had to do better, we had to react positively but maybe they didn't like hearing it. After losing all those games the morale was very low and everybody was depressed.

I was trying to inject some adrenaline, some life into the dressing room by getting people pumped up and angry again. Instead, it seems some of them complained to the manager and he decided it would be best to get rid of me as captain.

Advocaat told me a change of captaincy could make things better for the team. For once in my life I was totally lost for words.

He was droning on about how the Press was being very critical of me but I was coping with that because in my two-and-a-half years in Scotland there was always something being written about me, good and bad. I didn't pay any attention when I was getting praised and I tried not to notice when I was being criticised.

I could live with the Press but I think Advocaat was just using them as an excuse for doing what he was doing to me.

I told him that if he really felt that all Rangers' troubles would disappear the moment he took the armband off me, then fine, do it. I don't care.

But I did care. I cared more than he or anyone else could ever imagine but I wasn't going to give him the satisfaction of seeing how much he was hurting me.

I am a proud man just as a I was a proud boy in my home town of Bari. I would come home from school with cuts and bruises every week because I always stood up to boys who thought they could stand all over me.

Now this man was standing all over me and although I could not fight back, I was not going to let him see me cry. And I was crying inside.

He said to me: "I am going to make Barry Ferguson captain."

Now I really did think I was living a nightmare – and that is nothing against Barry, believe me.

I just could not believe that Advocaat was going to make a boy of Barry's age – he was 22 at the time – the captain of a club like Rangers. Barry was and is a very talented player but he was little more than a kid at the time and being the captain of an institution like Rangers is more than just leading the team out at three o'clock and tossing the coin.

It is a job for a man who has not only experienced football but experienced life. It is the same across the city with Celtic. I have not seen many boy-captains over there.

If Advocaat was going to strip me of the captaincy he had to go for someone with experience, surely. Someone like Jorg Albertz, for instance. Even Arthur Numan had been Advocaat's captain at PSV Eindhoven, so that would have made more sense than Barry.

He was too young. He had been playing regularly in our team for only 18 months and now suddenly he was to be made captain. I thought it was the wrong decision. I have nothing against Barry but at that time, in that period when the whole team was struggling, it was a lot to ask a boy to carry the burden of responsibility that being Rangers captain entails.

The pressure could have destroyed him but, thankfully, Barry has continued to progress as a player and he should be congratulated for that. But it could have gone the other way, and if it had, Advocaat would have ruined one of the best midfield players Scotland has produced in many years.

I think that when Advocaat really looks deep into himself he will know he did the wrong thing and I'll tell you why. We had won the league the season before by 21 points. We went on to lose the league to Celtic that season by 15 points.

Did we improve as a team by removing me from the captaincy? The league table never lies.

But Advocaat is not the kind of person who will admit he has made a mistake. Maybe not even to himself.

Don't get me wrong – I am not saying I was playing like Franco Baresi. I WASN'T playing well but, believe, me I wasn't the only one.

If Advocaat really didn't like how I was performing during that period why didn't he just say: "Lorenzo, I think you should take a rest and stay on the bench for a little while."

That would have been more acceptable. Instead I was made the scapegoat because I was the captain.

Thinking about this – and you can appreciate I have had plenty of time to do so over the last two years – I think Advocaat had another agenda that was served by throwing me to the lions. He was under intense pressure from the fans and the media because of our poor start to the season and after two seasons of almost unbroken success he didn't know how to handle it. One way to release the pressure was to shift the blame onto me and telling me I was no longer his skipper was the way he did it. Suddenly the newspapers were all Lorenzo, Lorenzo, Lorenzo ... not What's Gone Wrong with Advocaat?

I am sure that was his thinking: "If Lorenzo gets the blame I will save myself." And maybe, for a while, it worked.

It was also probably why he made a Scottish player the captain. He wanted to get the fans back on his side.

I remember making my way from his office down to the dressing room in a daze because I could not believe what I had just heard. Now we were going down to share the news with my team-mates.

I was very calm as he spoke to the players and told them that I was no longer the captain.

Remember, I had asked him to come to the dressing room to explain his system to the players? Well, all he did was say things we already knew: "I don't like how you are playing. You are well paid and have a good life, so you must do better."

We knew that. What we didn't know was how he wanted us to play on the pitch – and he didn't share that with us.

Advocaat finished that speech then said something that left me gasping with astonishment.

He told the players that he and I had come to a decision TOGETHER that I would no longer be the captain.

Now that was just a blatant lie but I had had enough by that time and just let him get on with it.

He asked if anyone had anything to say about it – he wanted to know who agreed and who disagreed. People like Jorg Albertz and Sergio Porrini were saying: "This is not fair, it is not right. You are basically saying that Lorenzo is taking the blame."

Stefan Klos had been away for a couple of days and when he

returned he came straight up to me and said: "I can't believe it, Lorenzo. You do not deserve this."

The Scottish players didn't say anything and neither did the Dutch. I think the Scots didn't say anything because they were happy to have a Scottish captain. They were protecting the Scottishness of the club and that's normal and understandable.

Why didn't the Dutch say anything? Because they are Dutch.

At the end of the day Advocaat took the decision and I was very upset. I never thought I could lose something so important to me.

I was not only the first foreign captain, I was the first Catholic captain and it meant everything to me.

In Scotland, actually in Britain as a whole, the people are very conservative and traditional. They don't like things to change very much from the past. There is nothing wrong with that point of view but when I was made captain everything changed for Rangers and it was a great honour for me.

I knew all about their tradition of not signing Catholic players until quite recently in their history and later in this book I will explain how I am able to deal with that situation.

All I will say at this point is that when I joined Rangers it was, and still is, a cosmopolitan club with the religion or colour of its employees meaning absolutely nothing. And that is how it should be and must be.

For all that though, nobody had ever made a Catholic the club captain and now not only were they getting a Catholic, they were getting an Italian Catholic! It made me immensely proud.

The best part for me was the feeling that I had come to a strange land, hardly knowing the language or the culture, and had adapted well enough for the people at the club to like and accept me so much that they wanted me to be the leader.

You don't get many foreign captains of clubs in this country. It is difficult to achieve but I had made it and it made my chest puff out. There were others who were probably ahead of me in the queue – I'm thinking of guys like Colin Hendry and Jorg particularly, as I had played very few games due to injury in my first season – and it meant the world to me and my family.

It was working great as well. The Treble in my first season with the armband, a Double in my second. Then Advocaat took it away from me and it was so unacceptable.

I didn't say much in the dressing room after the manager made his announcement and left. Nobody said much. I don't think the players knew where to look or what to say.

A few of my friends like Sergio, Jorg and Stefan had some words of comfort for me. I vaguely remember Tugay coming over and saying he was sorry for me but I was so numb that I have no real recollection of what was said.

I left the stadium in a bit of a daze but the initial hurt was soon elbowed aside by anger. How dare this man do this to me?

I called my agent Andreas D'Amico in Italy and I told him: "You have to get me away from here – I cannot accept what has happened."

I think Andreas was worried that I would do something stupid, like cause a big confrontation, but I was never going to do that. I was very calm but very determined that I had to leave Rangers after such a humiliation.

My first reaction, I must admit, was to tell Advocaat to stuff his team there and then. We had a game the following day against Dundee United in the CIS Cup and my first thought was to refuse to play if he picked me.

There was simply no point because he had blamed me for everything that had gone wrong. That hurt me so much because from the day I signed my contract for Rangers, I sweated blood for the club.

My first few months were ruined by injury – and again I will return to that time later – but I was totally committed to this club and I still am.

But for several months after Advocaat dropped that bombshell on me, I wanted out.

I gave him everything for two seasons, picking up five trophies, and he did not give me an ounce of respect back. How could I want to work with a man like that?

I will never forget it and to be honest, I will never forgive him. It was like being stabbed in the back.

Don't get me wrong – I am not saying Lorenzo was playing great and nothing was my fault. I know I wasn't at my best but there were outside influences that were affecting my performances. Maybe it is a surprise to people who don't play the game at this level just how much you can be affected if you have worries in your personal life.

Not long before, I had broken up with my girlfriend Cristina. She had come with me to Scotland and when she returned to Italy it affected me badly. Also, my mother was ill back home in Italy and it was so difficult being so far away from her and only being able to speak to her on the other end of a telephone line.

People think that footballers have a life of great riches and glamour. Being a player for a club like Rangers does reward you in those ways and we are lucky to be able to make a lot of money from the game, fortunate to live in lovely homes, buy expensive cars and designer clothes if we want.

But when your heart is aching it doesn't matter if you are a prince or a pauper.

To an outsider, I probably had everything. But I had very few people I could really talk to. It was a lonely and upsetting time.

On the day Advocaat dropped his bombshell, I had to get out

of Glasgow. I knew I could not go home and sit looking at four walls. I would have cracked up.

I have a very good friend who lives in Perth, Vito Laviola, to whom I was introduced by Andreas not long after I arrived in Scotland and we immediately hit it off. Maybe it was because, by coincidence, we were brought up in the same area of Italy, but it's probably just because he is a really good guy.

I called him and told him I was coming up to talk to him. We just chatted for hours and went for a long walk to clear my head. I couldn't have done that in Glasgow but Perth is a place where I had a little more space and on that day I needed it.

Vito organises hunting and shooting days in Perthshire for foreign visitors but when he saw the state I was in he took a few days off and came back to Glasgow with me.

He knew I didn't want to be alone when all this was going on. That was a kind and humanitarian gesture which meant the world to me.

My agent Andreas was another person I could talk to but he was in Italy. He told me not to do anything hasty because if I was to get a new club it would not be until the transfer window re-opened in Italy the following January.

He gave me advice I decided to follow. He said: "Lorenzo, play with your head up and your chest out. Play with dignity but play for yourself now. Play well every game and show people out there that you are a good player. That's what will get you a move when the time is right."

So, that's what I did. Before that day, I gave my heart and soul to Rangers. For a long, long time after it I played only for Lorenzo Amoruso.

I made another phone call that day and it was one of the most difficult I've ever made in my life. I had to tell my mum and dad that their boy was no longer the captain of Glasgow Rangers.

I had to tell them before they saw it in the newspapers. I knew the story would make headlines in Italy as well as in Scotland and if they saw that I had been sacked as captain they would think I must have done something very, very bad.

I had to get to them first and assure them that although I was being punished, I had done nothing wrong.

I was also worried that career-wise people would get the wrong impression. Other managers would see I had been stripped of the armband and think: "Maybe he's a bad influence."

It's the kind of thing that can destroy a career.

I rang home and my father picked up the phone. I said simply: "Listen dad, before you see the newspapers, I'm telling you I am no longer captain."

My dad was upset, I was upset. It was not the best telephone call of my life.

When I hung up though, my mood had changed again. I thought about Andreas' words and I decided that, yes, I still wanted away, but I was not going to hide. I was going to show everyone that I was still a very good football player.

I woke up the next morning and my first thought was: "Did I dream all that?" Unfortunately, I hadn't.

I went into the ground and, of course, the staff all knew what had happened by then. But they still couldn't believe it.

I remember our kit man Jimmy Bell looking completely stunned: "What happened? Why?" he asked me. I had no answer for him.

But with Andreas' advice ringing in my ears I played against Dundee United and we won easily, 2-0. Being in the dressing room before that game was a strange experience. I was very quiet, lost within myself really, and when it was time to leave the room and move into the tunnel I hung back. I wasn't going to go out second, behind the new captain.

So I let everyone go out the door before me and I chose to come out last. It was a weird night, you know, because the fans didn't seem to know how to take the news.

The news had come out that I was no longer the captain, so they were not expecting to see me lead the team out.

Some fans were singing: "There's Only One Amoruso", but others were chanting Dick Advocaat's name as well. I think they were in the same state of turmoil as the team. They weren't united, the team wasn't united – the whole thing was a mess but we still won the game.

I didn't really speak to Advocaat again properly. He would speak to me occasionally about how we would be playing on the Saturday and I would listen and talk to him when necessary. But only about the team – it was a very, very long time before we ever had a meaningful conversation again.

Advocaat did get some short-term respite from the pressure he was under – we hammered St Mirren 7-1 at Ibrox the following Saturday. Young Kenny Miller got five goals and at least the fans went home with a smile on their faces.

But reality was to slap us in the face again the following midweek and as usual, it hit me harder than the rest.

We played Monaco in a game we had to win to stay in the Champions League. I got caught in possession of the ball in midfield when we were winning 2-1 and Marco Simeone went on to equalise.

I got slaughtered in the Press for the loss of the goal but that didn't bother me as much as reading the criticism I received from Arthur Numan and Michael Mols.

I hold my hand up. I lost the ball but it was 50 yards from goal and there was time and players behind me to mop up the mistake. That didn't happen, Monaco scored and I was hung out to dry again.

I had seen the papers by the time I came into training the next day and I knew what Michael and Arthur had said. I decided to ignore them completely.

After a couple of days we were involved in a practice game and Arthur tried to tell me to do something. I looked at him and said: "Listen, you do your f****** business and I will take care of my business by myself."

He asked what was wrong and I replied: "You are still talking to me after what you said in the newspapers?"

Arthur tried to say he didn't say the things he was quoted as saying but every single newspaper had the same words – they didn't ALL make them up.

I just told him: "Remember, I am not the only one who goes on the pitch. This is a team sport and you think I am going to take all the blame. If I go down, I'm taking somebody else with me."

We were due to play Aberdeen away the following Sunday and on the day of the match I answered a knock on my hotel room door to find Arthur and Michael standing outside. "We want this sorted out," Arthur told me.

So they came into the room and both insisted they had been misrepresented in the Press. They didn't want a sour atmosphere in the dressing room and I understood that but, as far as I was concerned, the incident had happened and I had been made the scapegoat. They didn't apologise but they made it clear they wanted a united dressing room.

I don't know whether or not Advocaat had sent them in but in the end we all agreed just to get on with things. Arthur, Michael and I get on fine now but it was a difficult time.

That Aberdeen match was strange in many ways because I didn't think I was going to play. If that had happened then I might not be at Ibrox today.

The way Advocaat had set up training the day before the game made me think that I would be on the bench. If that had been the case then it was obvious that he, too, blamed me for the Monaco match.

If I was going to pay for it with my place in the team then I would have walked out on the club. I was feeling really low anyway having lost the armband and that would have been the final humiliation.

It wasn't good but by then I was thinking only of myself. Nobody at Ibrox was thinking about my welfare at that point and when everybody lets you down you become very defensive and adopt the mentality that you have to look after yourself because nobody else is going to do it for you.

I locked myself into my own little bubble and didn't let anybody get close to me after that. But, come the Sunday, I was named in the team after all and played really well as we beat Aberdeen.

My game improved because I was thinking only of myself. Rangers also benefited because if I was playing better, it had to help the team. But that wasn't my prime consideration. I was only looking after Lorenzo.

My form attracted the interest of a couple of clubs, however, and for a while I thought West Ham United were going to offer me an escape route from Ibrox.

About a month before the winter break their manager at the time, Harry Redknapp, made contact with my agent. He asked me to meet him and I told him I would be happy to talk to him if the clubs could agree a fee.

To be honest, playing and living in London was appealing and although things had settled down a little at Ibrox, I was still determined to move. There was a lot of chat between everyone involved and during the winter break Harry and his vice-chairman came over to meet me in Florence.

We spoke for two hours and I told him what I wanted and they told me what they wanted.

I wasn't asking for much more than I was getting at Rangers. I was only taking into account the cost of houses in London and Harry didn't think there would be a big problem, although he did say he wasn't getting on too well with his chairman.

I told him I wanted to come to Upton Park and that if he needed to know anything about me as a player or a person then he need only speak to Paolo di Canio. I am good friends with Paolo and I spoke with him about the move. As always, Paolo was super-enthusiastic. He just kept saying: "Come to West Ham, it will be great!"

But things dragged on a little then I heard that Harry had resigned as West Ham's boss. Obviously, he really wasn't getting on too well with his chairman!

After that short spell at home for the winter break the team gathered again in Glasgow before heading to Florida for training in the good weather.

I just got my head down and worked as hard as possible in the knowledge that I had to be fit and sharp if I was to get my move. I was still determined to go because although months had passed, I could not and would not forget what had happened.

Celtic were ahead of us in the league but the gap was not one that could not be closed. I think they were about eight points ahead and we had not given up hope. I was flying in training. My mind was the most positive it had been for a long time.

Then in the last five minutes of the last training session of the last day at the training camp in America, I pulled my hamstring. What a nightmare.

I returned depressed again and missed six games in a row as I waited for the muscle to heal. In that period we lost to Celtic in the CIS Cup semi-final and in the league at Parkhead. Both were in the space of a few days and the 1-0 loss in the league

25

more or less made it certain we would not catch the Hoops.

Eventually, I got back to fitness. Not long afterwards we went to play Dundee United at Tannadice in the Scottish Cup. But Rangers lost 1-0 and that was the end of our season. It was not even the middle of March and Rangers had lost everything.

I was really angry. On the way back to Glasgow I sat on the bus fuming because we did not create a single chance in that game. Our season was on the line but we had no creativity and no fight. I've said before – you can lose a football match, but you must lose with respect. That day I don't think we had any self-respect. The players were not committed to the manager.

The team had fallen apart and now we had about two months to go and nothing to play for. I had endured a lot of suffering in that season but that game made me feel just as bad in many ways as the other stuff that had gone on. There was just no spirit. It had all gone.

Advocaat's words on the day he took the armband away came flooding back into my head as we made our way home.

He had said: "I think that by taking away the captaincy we can make this team better. That is the most important thing."

It didn't happen. We got worse and worse and worse. And you know what? I honestly believe we handed Celtic the league the day he made that decision. Yes, we were already behind them but I can imagine them sitting in their dressing room at Parkhead and saying: "Look at the state of Rangers. They are all fighting among themselves.

"If they are changing captains they must have very big problems. We have got them on the run."

Celtic already looked like a compact, tight unit under Martin O'Neill in that first season he was there. I think that seeing us coming apart at the seams made them even more tight-knit. I think it was a major influence on the way the season developed.

Rangers lost everything. I lost the captaincy but I retained my self-respect and my dignity.

Anybody who knows me will realise that this was the biggest victory of all. It was a triumph for my determination not to be broken and the way I handled those few months is a monument to the way my mother and father brought me up in Bari.

It is time to introduce you to them.

# *Chapter Two*

## BROUGHT UP IN BARI

I ENTERED this world screaming and kicking on June 28, 1971. Some people would say I haven't stopped kicking since, but what do they know?

As most babies were in Italy at that time, I was born in my mum and dad's house in Palese, just five miles or so from the city of Bari in the south east of the country, around one hour's journey from our capital, Rome.

I was big and healthy at birth, around four kilos (8lb 8oz) in weight, and I think my mum Antonietta and dad Mauro were pleased that I was a boy because it completed the set – my sister Angelica had been born three years earlier. When I was six, a third baby was born into the Amoruso family – my wee brother Davide! We got on very well during our childhood days and still do. He is 25 now and works as a computer troubleshooter for one of the big banks back home.

Whenever their system crashes they call Davide and he sorts it out. He's a bright boy and luckily for him he has also inherited his big brother's good looks!

Actually, Davide could have followed my footsteps in becoming a professional footballer if it were not for some very bad luck when he was about 14.

He was an excellent player and was attracting the attention of some clubs when at that age he started having problems with his knees. I don't know if it was caused by playing too much football at a young age, but his knee-caps started to split and the bones would rub and scratch against each other.

Obviously, he was in a great deal of pain and distress and the doctors told him the problem could be solved only if he stopped punishing his legs by playing so much active sport.

It must have been heartbreaking for him – I know I would have been devastated if such a thing had ever been said to me – but Davide was left with no choice and for three years he did not kick a football. By the time his knees had recovered he was almost 18, he had lost too much time and could not be a professional player.

He is, however, a very intelligent young man who speaks very good English and has carved out a successful career for himself. We are very proud of him.

My sister, Angelica, is a lovely girl who is the only one of the three of us to have got married so far. Seven years ago she made my mum and dad, Mauro, the happiest people in the world when she gave them their first grandchild.

Arianna is the most beautiful niece an uncle could have and I love her to bits. My sister, brother and I were brought up in a loving environment but that doesn't mean to say that everything about it was easy. It wasn't.

We were happy but at that time in the 1970s, and still now to an extent, it is a hard life. The south of Italy is a lot less prosperous than the cities in the north such as Milan and Turin and the people have to work very hard just to make enough money to live on.

The Italians in general are very family-orientated and will do whatever is necessary to put food on the table for their children.

When I was growing up I remember it was almost impossible for most of the adults I knew to get a very good job. Most of the work was in the construction industry where men worked very long hours for very little pay.

They were paid what we called 'black money' – cash in hand – so that the employer and the worker didn't have to pay tax on it. There weren't a lot of big, big companies ploughing money into the area and it was a struggle for most people.

That was more than 20 years ago and thankfully things are changing, but there is still a north-south divide in terms of economic growth in Italy.

My dad used to work for a telephone company and believe me work is the correct word. He used to dig the trenches into which the telephone cables would go but when they broke he would get the call to come out and fix them.

It didn't matter where they were, he would have to sort out the problem. There were many times he would be soaked through because the cables were under water and he had to go down and fix them. It was very manual, very hard work and he could be called out at any time of the day or night.

I remember on many occasions hearing my dad climbing out of his bed at 3am because he'd had a call that a cable needed to be mended. There were times when we would not see him for three or four days because he had been called to another area and could not come home every night. He worked so hard for his family but he was also a traditional Italian father figure in that he did not want his wife to work to support the family.

So in all the time we were growing up, my mum was always the one who was at home to look after us. She was, however, an accomplished dressmaker and would sit at home doing this kind of work for people, but she didn't actually go out to work for someone else.

Between doing that, looking after three very active children and the house, she had a full-time job all right.

My dad was also absolutely determined that his three children should have a chance to get better jobs than he and most people around Bari had. He drilled into us the need to have a good education and to get the diplomas that would open the door to a better world. That, though, meant a lot of sacrifices for him.

To have three children stay at school for so long, when they could have been out working from the age of 15 or 16, meant that he had to keep providing the money to buy food and clothes. But we all got those diplomas and I think that made him very proud.

We didn't think like this at the time, I suppose, but when we look back there is also real pride in our hearts for the way my parents brought us up. They taught us right from wrong. They made us study for a better life and gave things up so that we would have a better chance of making it.

I have been lucky enough to make a very good living from football and the most joyful thing for me is now to be in a position where I can make my parents' life more comfortable. They did it for me when I was younger and now I am able to do it for them as they get a little older.

It was even harder for my dad back then because the Amorusos could not rely on the usual family support network that exists in Italy. I remember it being tough for him because he had no help. My grandpa on my dad's side of the family was already dead and there was a problem with my grandparents on my mum's side which meant we hardly ever saw them.

I suppose many families have fall-outs but we had this big, big mess-up and I heard them saying some very bad things about my family. I was young and could not forget what they said. Obviously, neither could my mum or dad because we did not see my grandparents again for many years.

That caused some sadness when I was growing up because all my friends had grandmums and grandads coming to visit them, taking them for ice creams and buying them toys, but ours never came and I didn't have that.

Many years later, we heard that my grandma was dying and my mum wanted to see her. She didn't drive so I took her and it is not easy for me to admit this, but I didn't feel anything for my grandma or grandpa.

It was as if they had never been part of my life so I could not suddenly switch on loving feelings for them. They were like strangers and, of course, that's really what they were because there had been no contact for so long.

I am only telling you this to underline how difficult it was for my parents. I owe them everything because they were unbelievable in the way they put themselves second behind their children. Always.

I cannot tell you when I first fell in love with football simply because there has never been a time when it wasn't in my heart. All my earliest recollections, from when I was about two years old, revolve around kicking a ball.

My mum is always saying that even when I was in her stomach I was kicking around so it has always been there. She has a picture of me when I was about 10-months-old with a football. I couldn't walk but I was trying to kick it about.

I always wanted to be a professional player. I wasn't like some kids who dreamed of being a doctor or a pilot. For me, football was everything. But I never left school because I wanted an education behind me and I wanted to learn about things other than football. It was all about improving myself.

I knew where I came from, but also that there was a big world out there away from the city boundary of Bari and that, one day, I would leave.

From very early on I made it a mission in my life to earn a lot of money so that I could pay back my parents for what they had given me. I don't know why that feeling was so strong inside me but I still feel like that – even at 31. Maybe I was over-mature for my age but I saw the sacrifices they were making and for me it was vital that someday I could repay them.

It makes me proud that I have been able to do this. They are not flashy people who want big cars and things like that. But they deserve to be able to see out their days without wondering where the next meal is coming from.

My dad retired from his job not so long ago and like many people of his age – mid 60s – the shock of not having to get up to go to work after having done so for so long, affected him badly. He changed a lot and I was quite worried about him.

He was very bored having so much time on his hands so I came up with an idea to get his mind and body active again. I bought him a plot of land not far from our home and suggested he grow vegetables on it.

You should see this piece of earth now – it is a paradise with the most luscious tomatoes, potatoes, fruit … everything! He loves it and when we are back home together for family gatherings you can see the delight on his face as we all sit down to eat the vegetables he has produced.

Even at this stage in his life my dad is still putting food on the table for us. He and my mum are happy and that is the most important thing for me. But I like to see everybody happy although I know that is not possible all the time. It is the reason why I like doing some charity work or signing autographs and posing for pictures with people.

It doesn't take much out of my day to do this and if it means a lot to them, then why not? A lot of people have said to me: "You've made my day today," just because I had my picture taken with them.

That seems strange because to me. I am just Lorenzo. But if it makes them happy then that's great. It doesn't cost me a penny to sign an autograph or to smile for a camera and it is something I enjoy.

Of course, being asked for autographs and such-like was a long way away as I took my first steps on the road to adulthood at the age of five when I enrolled in the Scole Elementare Lovengine – my primary school. I had been at the equivalent of nursery school before that, but this was the real thing.

And it wasn't easy for me because suddenly I was thrust into this place where all the children were older and bigger than me. They tried to pick on the younger ones who had just joined, including me, and that meant a lot of heartbreak because I would always fight back – and most of the times I would come off worst. At least at first I would.

The teachers were always complaining about me because I would not let anyone step on me. Not a chance. So almost every day my mum would pick me up from school and give me a hard time because I would have a cut lip or a bruised eye or my clothes would be ripped.

This went on for most of my young school life. I still studied well but my refusal to allow anyone to bully me or try to knock me about meant that a fair amount of trouble followed me around.

My parents were a little bit worried but, looking back, I was just an ordinary street boy getting into scrapes that most kids of that age do. We were always playing football in the streets – that's just a way of life in Italy. People tell me that it used to be the same in Scotland but I don't see much evidence of it now to tell you the truth.

Maybe kids here have too many Playstations and things to take their minds off football. It seems logical to me that the more children who are encouraged to play the game from an early age, the more good players will develop.

Anyway, when we weren't playing football we'd be climbing trees or stealing fruit from them. Even roses! But that was a very clever ploy by young Lorenzo, you know. When I knew my mum was annoyed with me – maybe I had been in another fight or was going to arrive home later than I had been told to by her – I would always bring her a big bunch of roses which I had picked from a garden on the way home.

She knew I didn't have the money to buy them and would look at me funny then break into a big smile and give me a hug.

But generally my friends and I were good boys but pretty wild. I always had scars and cuts from falling from trees – myself and a couple of friends made a brilliant tree house one summer and it was so high that we were the only ones who dared climb up to it. It was a great time and although I had my falls and accidents, thank God I never had a serious injury that landed me in hospital. No broken legs or arms, thankfully.

By that time I was not only playing football for the school but also handball, basketball and volleyball – any sport with a ball had me volunteering to play it. I also ran for the school at longer distance events.

But although I threw myself into these activities, my father's advice was never far from the front of my mind. I knew my studies had to come first. The teachers were quite surprised by how well I did because a lot of the boys who were good at sports were not so good academically. But I was lucky to have a very good memory and after reading something only once or twice it would be lodged in my brain.

I still have that skill but back then it was very helpful because it meant I could play football for three hours then need only one hour's studying because I could learn whatever I had to in that time.

Like most things in my life, my football was influenced by my dad. He used to take a youth team on a Sunday and one of the guys on that team became a trainer himself after a few years.

When I was six, my dad asked me if I wanted to play for a team and, of course, my answer was yes. He took me to this guy, his name was Pasquale Fiorentino, and I trained with him and his team almost every day for the next five years.

The team was called Cucine del Levante – Cucine is Italian for kitchen and this team were sponsored by a local kitchen manufacturer. Pasquale is still chairman of this club down there and I saw him recently when I was home visiting my parents. It is a friendship that will never die.

I played there until I was 12 years old when my home-town team Bari discovered me. At that time I was a midfield player and sometimes a striker, because I had quite a good shot and scored a lot of goals.

Bari watched me a few times and made the decision to sign me – but my dad wasn't very happy about that. At the time they were not a very good club, they were in Serie B, and they did not have a great reputation. Dad was particularly concerned because he had been told their youth set-up was not the best.

At the same time another club was showing an interest in putting me into their youth development programme and only geography killed off something that would have been a dream for me. The club was Inter Milan, one of the most famous in Italy, and any youngster would have been desperate to join them. Me, perhaps, more than any of them because although

Bari was my local team I supported Inter from afar and would have loved the chance to play for them.

But Milan is more than 1,000 kilometres from Bari and there was no way my parents would consider letting their 12-year-old boy move so far away from home. That is understandable now but at the time I wasn't so considerate. I was inconsolable!

So I signed for Bari and began the slow process of moving through their age groups. At the age of 14 we were playing in Naples and straight after the game a guy approached me and my manager asking if I was interested in going to Florence to play for the international team at Under-15 level. I was amazed – I didn't even know there was an Under-15 national team!

I went to Florence where the Italian national football training centre, known as Coverciano, is based and I was immediately knocked out by just how beautiful the city was. Florence still takes my breath away whenever I go back there and, of course, at that time I was not to know that I would later make the place my home for two seasons when I signed for Fiorentina.

Walking through Coverciano was so exciting for this young boy who had football coursing through his veins. You walk through a corridor called the Temple of Football and you see all these pictures of the great Italian players and teams of the past.

I was just 11 when Italy won the 1982 World Cup in Spain and this was just a couple of years later. There were pictures of that success everywhere and it made it all seem so much more real to be here in this place where my heroes had walked over the years. It was an unbelievable feeling.

There were 50 boys involved in this get-together which amounted to a trial for the Under-15 team. In a game we had I scored two goals – one an unbelievable strike – so I was feeling really good. Then, near the end of the game, I did something to my shoulder. I damaged the nerves in it and could not play football for three weeks. The first international of the season was coming up the following week so my chance had gone.

But I came back for the next session and eventually got my chance. We had to travel to Switzerland, which was very exciting for me, and we won the game 4-1. My family was bursting with pride at the thought of their son representing our country and what made it even better was that I was one of three guys from the south of Italy to have made the team. The rest were from Rome and to the north of the capital.

That was the first time the newspapers did an article on me and it was so exciting to see my name in print. It's funny how you get used to it over the years but in the beginning it was great.

While all this was going on, I never left school. But it was getting more difficult to combine everything I was doing with my studies. I would be going away for three or four days with the football squad then return to school tired. Inevitably the studies suffered.

I was at high school in Bari by this time – about 10 miles from the family home in Palese. Every morning I woke up at 6.30am to catch a train to Bari at 7.30am which got me to the city at 8am, half an hour before lessons started.

We finished school around 1.30pm then I had to walk or take a bus to the city centre, where I caught another bus to the opposite side of the city where Bari trained. The training would finish at 5pm or 6pm then I would have to make the journey in reverse. I would get home between 7.30 and 8pm, absolutely shattered. I would grab a bite to eat then sit down to study.

When I was finished with that, it would be time to go to bed then, first thing next morning, I would go through the same routine all over again.

This happened for five years and it did take its toll. I was mentally and physically exhausted and one day my body simply packed in, giving everyone around me the fright of their lives.

Me? I wasn't frightened. That's because I was out cold and completely unaware of what had happened.

As well as playing football for my school I also represented it at volleyball and handball. It was during a volleyball match that my body screamed at me a warning I could not ignore.

I just remember moving towards the ball then ... nothing. My body and my brain had flicked off and I collapsed onto the floor unconscious. After I don't know how long, I gradually became aware of people crowding me in, then slowly and hazily I began to come round.

I'll never forget the look on my team-mates' faces and the teachers as well – when they saw me faint so suddenly, they were convinced I was dead.

I was taken to the hospital where blood tests and many other examinations were given to me in an attempt to work out why I had passed out so suddenly. My parents, sister and brother were worried sick because they did not know if something serious was wrong or if it was just a one-off occurrence.

Thankfully the tests showed it was just that – a one-off. But it could develop into something more dangerous if I continued to live life at 100mph. The doctors told me I would be okay but that I was overworking myself. If I did not stop exerting myself so much, the consequences could be very serious.

They kept me in hospital overnight just to be sure that nothing bad would happen and next day I was allowed to go home – but it had been an alarm call that I could not ignore.

I knew I could not give up my football. I knew that my studies were vital to me. So the handball and the volleyball stopped there and then. I was still leading a busy life but at least now I was giving my body the odd break now and again.

That incident was the second major scare I had given my parents. When I was 12 years I almost drowned. In fact I was convinced I was dead, and I experienced something that to this day I have never been able to explain.

Bari is a seaside town and a bunch of us youngsters sometimes went swimming and diving for seafood and shells which we would collect then sell for some extra pocket money.

One very windy day a group of us were doing this but the sea was very rough and it was not easy. Then suddenly this huge wave smashed straight into my face, sending me spinning and knocking me senseless.

I was swallowing water – huge mouthfuls of it – and panicked because I didn't know where the surface was. The seabed was very rocky rather than sandy and I know my head smashed against it. Then I drifted out of consciousness.

You've heard the expression that your life flashes before you, well it really did happen to me. I don't know what happened then but I felt myself swimming against the current, although I knew I didn't have the strength to do it.

The next thing I knew I was lying on the beach, my eyelids were fluttering open and bright sunlight flooded in. The face of a lady filled my vision. Except, there was no lady on the beach – only my friends who were crowding over me as I retched and vomited. I asked my friends if there had a been lady around at all and they said no. Was it a vision? A religious sighting? I honestly don't know. I only know it happened.

I was lucky that day but it was a tragedy six years later when I was 18 that really made me think hard about life. One of my best friends – I won't name him out of respect for his family – was an expert swimmer and diver. He used oxygen tanks, the whole works, and practically lived in the sea.

One day he went diving and something happened to him out there. His body was found two or three days later. I was utterly devastated. I remember thinking: "Why did I survive all those years ago when my friend, who was better prepared and a better swimmer, died?"

I still think about it often and still don't have the answer.

By the time of my volleyball scare, when I was 16, I was fully involved with Bari's first-team squad, which meant I never went to school on Saturdays because the squad trained during the mornings.

My teachers and headmaster were brilliant with me, though. They knew I wanted to study hard but they also recognised I had given myself a chance to make it as a professional footballer and they didn't discourage me from taking that route in life.

Throughout my youth career I always played with boys older than myself. At 13 I would be in the Under-15 team, for instance. By the time I reached 16, I was playing for Bari's Under-18 team but, more importantly, I was able to train with the first-team players.

Another significant change took place at this time. I was converted from a midfield player who could score a few goals to a defender whose job it was to stop others from doing so.

I was playing for the Under-18s although I was two years younger and the manager, Pasquale Loseto, had a few injured players and needed a centre-half one day. I was asked to play there because I was big and strong for my age. I did so, although at first I was not really happy there.

It took me a while to adjust but the fact that Loseto was a centre-half during his own playing days was a big help. I got a lot of personal coaching from him and gradually I found my feet at the back.

Loseto was a great encouragement to me and maybe he saw something in me that I hadn't seen in myself at that stage. He kept telling me: "Lorenzo, you can make it as a central defender. You've got everything you need to play in this position."

So I would play with the Under-18s and train with the first-team stars every day. It was unbelievable. I would be walking around with my eyes like saucers seeing all these great players going through their routines. I watched and learned.

Funnily enough, there were two British players there at the time and one of them, Paul Rideout, went on to play for Rangers later in his career. The other, Gordon Cowans, played for Aston Villa and England and he had a wonderful left foot.

The reaction of my friends to the news that I was training with the first-team was funny. They simply didn't believe me.

I would tell them: "I was training with the first-team today," and you would look at them and see they doubted my word. Why? Because on a Sunday when the first-team played, I was not in the team or on the bench.

I could not prove it to them but in the last two games of that season I made it onto the bench twice and although I didn't actually get on the pitch, at least my friends could see that I was telling the truth. I really was a Bari player!

Cowans and Rideout were leaving the club after that last game of the season, away to Padova, and I went to wish them all the best. Cowans told me: "Lorenzo, if you keep working as hard as you have been with us you will be a good footballer."

It's funny that I got this advice from British players when the Italians said nothing like this.

I finally made my first-team debut in the Italian Cup the following season. We played a small team called Barletta, who are based near Bari, so it was a bit of a derby and we won 3-0.

My first game in Serie B was against Parma and we won 2-1. I came on from the bench when we were 2-1 up and I was pleased with my performance.

I think it also made people sit up and take notice of me for the first time. If that was good, what was to follow just a couple of weeks later was the stuff that dreams were made of. We were drawn at home to Napoli in the next round of the Italian Cup and at the time they had Diego Maradona playing for them.

I could hardly sleep in the run-up to the game. Here was I, a 17-year-old who had idolised the Argentinian, getting the chance to play on the same field as him and, more than that, having to stop him scoring.

Actually, I was on the bench and before the game there is a warm-up area where players can do their own thing before running out onto the pitch. I crept out to see what Maradona was doing. He was past his peak by then but was practically making the ball sit up and talk to him. My eyes were popping out of my head and I just prayed with all my heart that I would have the opportunity to get on.

My prayers were answered with 20 minutes to go. It had been an incredible performance from us and we were 2-0 up so the manager wanted another defender on to make it harder for Napoli to get back into the game. So on I went and I remember making a couple of challenges on the great man. They didn't score and the match ended 2-0. I was ecstatic.

Afterwards, I knocked on the Napoli dressing room and shyly asked Maradona for his autograph. He signed, of course, and I still have it in my parents' home in Bari.

Up until then I was just another face in the crowd as I walked the streets of Bari. But almost overnight that changed. Footballers are treated like huge celebrities in Italy and all of a sudden I would notice people looking at me, then looking away, then looking again, as I went about my business. It took a lot of getting used to.

Obviously I am used to it now but back then I had to laugh about it. I would see them nudging each other and whispering: "That's Lorenzo – he plays for Bari." And I'm thinking: "So what?"

But secretly I was very happy. I was beginning to see that, yes, football could give me a life that was not just an ordinary existence.

There was another major bonus that came with being a recognised football player in Bari. Girls.

Before I got in the first-team, I was a nobody. Now I was a somebody. My face hadn't changed, my hair hadn't changed. But suddenly girls wanted to talk to me. Did I like this change in my circumstances? I was a red-bloodied teenage Italian boy so I will allow you to make up your own mind!

At about this time I was finishing at my high school but I still had a year to go to get my diploma, which meant going to another school. My teachers had told me I could choose whichever school I wanted because I had worked hard in difficult circumstances.

My idea was to get my diploma, then use it to go to university to become a sports teacher. I think in Britain, a P.E. teacher is the closest thing to it.

There was a college in Bari which allows people to train to become elementary – primary – school teachers over four years, so I went there.

As luck would have it, most people who want to be elementary teachers are girls and it was unreal.

There were about 1,000 pupils in this school. Around 930 of them were girls which made the 70 boys there very happy indeed. And very popular. It was like being inside the biggest sweet shop in Italy.

The fact that my picture was getting into the newspaper now because I was a Bari player didn't do me any harm either. It was murder – honestly!

In the last two years of this school – I would be maybe 19 by this time – we had to go out into schools to teach the youngsters. Although I was interested in being a sports teacher we had to cover a variety of subjects. I remember one day it was my turn to take a class and I was standing at the front giving my speech about what I wanted them to do and I noticed a young boy sitting about two rows back.

He kept looking at the palm of his hand, then his head kept shooting up and he would stare at me very hard. Then his eyes would flick back to his hand, then at my face again.

This went on for a while and after I had finished my speech I asked the class: "Guys, do you have any questions for me?"

This boy was out of his chair like a shot. He stood up and asked: "Is this you? Is this you? This is you, isn't it?"

Then he showed me the Panini sticker he'd had folded into the palm of his hand. It was indeed me and before the morning was out the entire school knew that the new trainee teacher was a Bari player.

From that day on I was a hopeless teacher because all every kid wanted to talk to me about was football. It was a lot of fun, though.

On a more serious note, it was getting more difficult for me to get my diploma because football was now eating into so much of my time. But I didn't give up. The college bent over backwards to accommodate me because they knew I didn't want to throw four years of studying in the bin. Between us we came to agreements about fitting in my lectures and study periods at times when I was not travelling all over the place with my football.

The time came for the final test and although I had studied like a demon in the last few weeks, I was still behind my fellow students because of the hours I had missed in previous years.

But the exam came, I sat it and, to my absolute delight and maybe just a little surprise, I passed. I had my diploma which allowed me to teach sport if my football career did not work out. Which for a while looked very possible. The following season in Serie B I played only about eight games with Bari. Not that the team missed me much – we were promoted to Serie A and the prospect of playing against the big boys was tremendously exciting.

It wasn't long before reality hit me hard, though. If I didn't get many games in Serie B I got even fewer in the top league. I played four times but, as the team was struggling, I was expecting more. But even though the results were bad the manager, Gaetano Salvemini, wouldn't play me and I was getting very frustrated.

I did play in one match, which we lost, and the following week he took me out of the team. Me and nobody else. I thought that was a sign that he blamed me for the defeat so we had strong words.

I thought he was picking on me because I was the youngest player in the team and I wouldn't fight back. He was wrong – I have a tongue in my head and I was ready to use it. To be honest, I was very nasty to him. I said some things that should not have been said but the main thrust of my argument was that he took the easy way out by dropping me and not any of the bigger names, the bigger earners at the club.

The argument cost me dear, however, because I didn't play for Bari in the remaining six months of that season. The year after I was shipped out on loan – and what a culture shock that was for a Serie A player who, by that time, was playing at Under-21 level for the Italian national team.

I was sent to the Third Division to play for Mantova in the north of the country near Parma. It was a slap in the face. Not because they were not good people there, because they were. But being loaned to any team in the Third Division would be an insult to a player who reached my level.

It was a big, big blow to me. Very few people would watch their games and the level of football was completely different. It was one of the strangest periods, not only of my career, but of my life.

When I was at Bari, I was always surrounded by people who

said they were my friends. But I quickly learned that they just liked the idea of hanging around with footballers. There was me thinking they were close to me because I was a good guy, but that was maybe just my youthful naivety showing through.

As soon as I went to play in the Third Division most of these people disappeared in a flash. Only a few remained but those were the ones I knew were my real friends. It was a harsh lesson but one I have never forgotten. And in many ways it was a good thing because it helped me identify who I could trust.

Being loaned out to Mantova meant having to live away from home for the first time in my life and I did not find it easy. But I played well there, as I should have because it was the Third Division, and returned to Bari the following summer hoping for a fresh start.

The club had been relegated back to Serie B while I was away and it was intimated to me that when I came back I would be given the chance of a regular run in the team.

So I went back, but I don't know why. I didn't get a chance. Not even in the friendlies before the league got under way. And with the season just two months old I was shipped out on my travels again – this time on loan to a Second Division club Pesaro, which played in the league below Bari.

I had a great season there and, in my heart of hearts, I did not feel I would ever again play for Bari because they had humiliated me by their treatment.

A couple of Serie B teams had noticed my performances for Pesaro and wanted to buy me but Bari failed to get promoted that season and didn't want to sell me to a rival.

But Bari changed manager and when they did everything changed for the better. Guiseppe Materazzi came in and said: "Why should I have to buy a good defender when I have Lorenzo Amoruso? I want him back."

Initially I told him I didn't want to come back but Materazzi told me this was a fresh beginning. There were new people at the top of the club. There was a new manager and he would be bringing in new players.

He promised me a new start and his enthusiasm and persuasiveness was seductive. Also, I was still under contract so I had no real choice. I returned to Bari to try again.

This time it was to be different. At the age of 22, my career, which had stalled like a Formula One car on the starting grid at a Grand Prix, was finally about to take off.

It was to be a high octane ride that would lead me all the way to Glasgow via Florence.

# *Chapter Three*

## STEPPING INTO THE BIG TIME

UNLIKE most of his predecessors at Bari, Materazzi was as good as his word and I responded to his honesty and to the faith he showed in me. We all did.

The manager created almost a completely new team and he was shrewd enough to bring in players from the Second and Third Division in whom he had spotted the potential to play at a higher level.

Most importantly though, each of the eight new boys - and I included myself in that number because for the past two seasons I had hardly considered myself to be a Bari player, having been shipped out to other clubs like some sort of slave - had a hunger and desire to succeed.

There are times when a manager goes the other way and buys guys who have played for years at the top level and don't quite have the legs or the lungs for that standard any longer. A manager will sometimes think: "Well, they can still do a job for me at this level", but I don't think that works very well.

First, it is a short term strategy because if those players do help you get promotion they have already said they are no longer good enough to play in the top division by coming to your club in the first place so they'll have to be replaced.

That's IF they get you promoted. It is more likely, though, that they won't have the drive and desire to push themselves and their team-mates if they've already seen it all and done it all earlier in their career. By then they will have been well paid for years and they'll look at moving to a smaller club as merely a way of topping up their retirement funds.

Maybe that's what Materazzi was thinking as well because he ignored that type of player and preferred to trawl the lower leagues looking for young, eager players with points to prove and fire in their bellies. To his credit he found them and he moulded them into a team at Bari during the last year of my contract.

Nobody gave us a chance of going up that season for the very reason I have just given you - nobody had heard of any of us. But we fought like fury every time we went onto the park, we ran until our opponents could run no more, and we won game after game.

Serie B was not an easy division to get out of, not with teams of the stature of Fiorentina in there with us, but we made it. We finished runner-up to the Florence club and the town celebrated as if we had won the Champions League itself.

I loved it. For the first time in all my years at Bari I really felt as if I belonged and like I had made a contribution. So when they asked me to sign a new contract I did so in the knowledge that this time I would get the chance to play in Serie A.

Materazzi added another couple of players to the team but there were still no star names. So just like the previous season nobody gave us a chance of living very long in the Italian top flight. We were the favourites to go straight back down but we had other ideas.

We were still young, still hungry, and we did unbelievably well. We won six matches away from home which in Italy is really difficult to do. And it wasn't just other small teams we beat either. Not unless you consider AC Milan, Inter Milan and Lazio to be small teams.

We beat the two Milan clubs in the San Siro and Lazio in the Olympic Stadium, Rome, as well as three smaller clubs. Talk about living in a dream! I know exactly how the Chievo players must have felt in Italy last season because their story is similar to ours although they took it a stage further by qualifying for the UEFA Cup which was an astonishing achievement for a club of its size.

The secret to our success was our fitness. I have never experienced a pre-season like the one Materazzi put us through. He knew that many clubs in Serie A had better quality players than Bari but he was determined to make sure that none of them had fitter players than he did. I think he succeeded.

He would take us into the hills that surround Bari and have us running up them at full pace 20 times in one session. One particular hill was really tough and you could hear the sound of people throwing up behind you as you ran up as fast as you could, heart pumping and head pounding in the oppressive heat of the summer.

We called that place Vomit Hill. I don't think I need to explain any further.

But the bottom line is that it was worth it because we didn't stop running all the way through the season. We won games we would have lost if it had not been for the incredible level of fitness we had.

With five games to go before the end of the season we had guaranteed our safety which wasn't bad for a team that the experts predicted would be relegated by March.

I had also proved a lot to myself and others by performing consistently well against some of the best strikers in the world and that had not gone unnoticed by bigger clubs.

Parma and Fiorentina made their interest known and I was aware that going to either of them would have been a significant step up the career ladder.

Parma told me they wanted me but they would have to wait a little while before making an offer to Bari. I don't know if they had to sell a player before they could buy but they were not ready to do a deal immediately.

Fiorentina, on the other hand, were very keen to get me in their jersey as soon as possible and I was impressed by how much they seemed to want me.

Their manager at the time was a man who was later to become very well known in Britain. Claudio Ranieri, now the manager of Chelsea, made me a very good offer and the fact that he was also keen to sign one of my very best friends and Bari team-mate, Emiliano Bigica, made it even better.

Bari accepted a combined bid of £6m for us both, we were on our way in our minds, if not immediately in our bodies.

The reason for that was that the deal was struck in May when there were still two league games to be played for Bari before our transfer was completed.

It was a great move for us both but Bari wanted the money more than we wanted to leave, to be honest. Emiliano and I went to the chairman and said: "If you can give us both a little more money we will stay and help Bari fight for a UEFA Cup place next season."

But the reply left little doubt that we would be playing our football in Florence the following season. He said: "Boys, I cannot turn down the money they want to give me for you. This money will help the club survive."

Emiliano actually accepted his contract right away but I had a little problem with mine. I had agents involved while Emiliano didn't. But Fiorentina wanted to give me exactly the same money as he was going to get. I told them that I had to pay my agents as well and wanted more money to enable me to do this.

Obviously they didn't agree immediately and we spoke on the phone for two or three days trying to get the problem resolved. Finally they agreed that Fiorentina would pay the agents and I would have the same contract as Emiliano.

I flew to Rome Airport to meet Fiorentina's people and we signed the contract there before going our separate ways again because I still had two games to play for Bari before the end of the season.

We got the first of those games played without any problems but just before the final match the newspapers got wind of the fact that Emiliano had agreed to sign for Fiorentina. Until then nobody knew anything because Bari had asked Fiorentina to keep it secret as they knew the fans would go crazy if it came out that the club was selling two of its best players.

Bari wanted the deal to come to light in the close season, allowing the fans time to have calmed down by start of the new campaign.

It didn't work out like that though. The Press got half the story and luckily for me, it was Emiliano's half.

They wrote that Bigica had signed for Fiorentina but there was no mention of Amoruso in the story. I was delighted and as soon as we walked onto the pitch for our last game it was clear why I had reason to be so happy about it.

The crowd was going absolutely crazy and they were calling poor Emiliano every bad name you can think of. He was jeered whenever he touched the ball and that was terrible because he had always given everything for the club. The general feeling was that he had betrayed Bari, which was untrue because the club wanted the money for him.

During the warm-up he came up to me saying: "You b*****d - you've done the same as me yet they still love you!"

But I know I would have got the same treatment if the fans had known that I was also going to Florence after this game.

We actually lost that last game, to Sampdoria but I scored a brilliant goal from a free kick. I knew it would be my last goal for the club even if the fans didn't and it was a special way to sign off.

With it being the end of the season the fans stayed at the end to cheer the team off in recognition of their efforts throughout the year. They were patting me on the back and all I could think was: "They'd kill me if they knew I was leaving."

The next day it was announced officially that I would be joining Emiliano in Florence and the supporters were up in arms about it. They complained to the club and to the newspapers but as there were no more games to be played that season they could not gather together to have a go at me.

The last game of the season was played on the Sunday and the next day we flew to Florence for the signing Press conference. It took us only minutes to realise we had entered another world from Bari.

We had moved from a small town to a beautiful, bustling, busy city and having experienced a little of it when I was a boy at the Coverciano I knew this was a place I would fall in love with.

That was off the pitch. Playing for Fiorentina was also going to be a completely different experience because this was the big-time. Suddenly everybody was interested in you. At Bari we had to deal with only three or four reporters who covered most of our matches.

When Emiliano and I turned up for the Press conference to announce our signing we got the shock of our lives. It seemed like a thousand people had packed into the hotel. Hundreds of flash-bulbs were popping and everyone was asking questions at the same time. It was like a night at The Oscars and it was both frightening and exhilarating at the same time.

Before meeting the Press we spent about 20 minutes with the chairman, Cecchi Gori, who struck me as being a very ambitious man. But that type can also be ruthless and it struck me that he might that kind of chairman.

With me though, he was fine. I had no problems with him.

Then there were the radio, television and newspaper interviews and right away I realised that Emiliano and I were going to have prove ourselves as worthy footballers all over again.

The tone of the questioning was not nice and the insinuation was that we would both struggle in Florence because we had come from a small club and would not be able to handle the pressure of playing for a big-name team.

They told us that it was one thing to be playing for a team that considered a success to be any season in which they weren't relegated, and another to play for one who felt it had failed if it did not at least make the UEFA Cup.

Those people had short memories, I thought. It was only the season before the previous one that both Fiorentina and Bari were in Serie B.

But that said, I knew that this was a big club and I was delighted to be there and absolutely determined to ram the doubts of the critics straight down their throats.

We told them that we wouldn't shout about what we were going to do. We would show them on the pitch.

The Press had judged us even before we'd kicked a ball for our new club but I think we handled the situation well. I'm even better at dealing with the media now, I believe, but then I've had to get better at it since moving to Scotland where everything I do is scrutinised.

In Italy there are two or three newspapers which deal exclusively with sport. The world might be ending tomorrow but it won't get a mention in La Gazzetta dello Sport or Corriere dello Sport but if Alessandro del Piero stubs his big toe on the pavement there will be two pages written about it.

They are very, very critical of players and clubs when things don't go right and they believe that because footballers in Italy earn so much money we are fair game.

The players and management all know that if they play even one bad game they will receive no mercy from the newspapers.

But here, more than in Italy, the gossip is unreal. The Press here turn any small thing into a big story and I am talking about at the front of the newspaper, not the back where you find the sports stories.

Unless you are a very important person in Italy you don't get that sort of treatment but in Britain, not just Scotland, it seems that every footballer can be on the front pages for very little reason. There is an obsession with celebrities that you just don't find in Italy and it takes a long time to get used to. In fact, after more than five years in Scotland, I admit I still can't get my head around it.

It is very difficult to explain what it is like to have your private life talked about so openly in public.

When I broke up with my girlfriend Cristina it was very big news in Scotland for days and there were photographs all over the papers.

All I can say is: "Why?" People split up with their girlfriends every day in life. It happens to just about every person at some point or other in their life. Why should this be such big news? I honestly do not understand it. Surely, there are much more important things to put in newspapers than Lorenzo Amoruso splitting up with his girlfriend.

In Italy I could walk through the city streets with my arm round my ex-girlfriend's shoulder and nobody would take a picture of us. But there have been several times I have been walking with a girl in Glasgow city centre and I have spotted photographers taking pictures from a distance.

I don't like it. In fact, I hate it.

It's difficult enough to have a normal life so when you get a day off you want to go to a nice place for lunch, or a stroll in the city, or spend some time shopping just to relax.

People kind of put you in a compartment when you are a footballer. They think that's what you do 24 hours a day and they forget that in reality we are still fairly young boys who have lives outside their work just as anyone else does.

We are under pressure for nine months a year - and I accept we are very well paid to handle it - but nevertheless we should be allowed some space and time to be people rather than footballers.

But that's life in Britain I suppose. I live here and I earn a good living here so I cannot expect every aspect of my life here to be perfect and I have to just get on with it.

I can't go up to a photographer and tell him: "F**k Off" because that just makes things worse. Then his newspaper has a picture of an angry Lorenzo shouting at their photographer, so it is better just to try to ignore it. But sometimes it is difficult, believe me.

Now I prefer not to go out in Glasgow because you don't get that kind of hassle in places like Perth or Dundee. I enjoy the countryside anyway, so getting away from it all does me good. And walking in the countryside with a set of golf clubs over my shoulder is one my favourite past-times, so escaping the paparazzi has done wonders for my handicap!

It is funny when people outside Glasgow see me because they are not like Glaswegians. They are not so forward and they will look but not approach you so readily. Glasgow people can be very funny. They are not shy, that's for sure and most of them are absolutely brilliant but with the Rangers-Celtic rivalry so intense you must always be on your guard because you just never know if something can flare up. If it did you can bet your life it would end up in the papers so I am always a little on edge in that kind of situation.

But in Italy the newspapers are far more clear cut. They believe that because you earn a lot of money you deserve the criticism if you play badly. They are not nearly as interested in your private life.

On the day I signed for Fiorentina, there seemed to be hundreds of Press there and fans as well. It showed me that the people of Florence were really crazy about their team. Their passion was unbelievable and being a one-team city everybody focused their attention on the football club.

Over the last few years Fiorentina has suffered terrible financial problems which culminated in it being declared bankrupt last season. The team was scrapped and a new Fiorentina was born but was made to play in the Third Division. It's incredible to think something like that has happened - it's the equivalent of, say, Tottenham Hotspur being shoved into the bottom English league.

They had to bring in a new team because all of the players, apart from one of the big names, Angelo di Livio, were sold.

Despite that happening to Fiorentina more than 16,000 of their fans bought season tickets to watch them in the Third

Division. That's incredible. Their first game at home was watched by 35,000 people and it proves that they will stick by their team no matter what.

But when I joined in 1995 the club was on the crest of a wave. And I took to playing and living in Florence like a duck takes to water.

I left Bari with the conviction that Florence was going to be a big step forward for me as a club and as a lifestyle. It is a beautiful city. Tourists swarm there for the history, for the art and for the architecture and I love the vitality it has.

The culture of the people is different from what I had been used to as well. Bari was a seaside city. Florence, although not far from the sea, is an inland city and is surrounded by beautiful hills.

I also met at this time a man who was to become a major influence in my life over the seven years I was lucky enough to know him.

His name was Father Giancarlo Setti, a Florentine priest, whom I was introduced to through another priest who used to come to Fiorentina matches and was almost like the equivalent of a club chaplain.

From the moment we met, we just clicked. He was someone I could talk to about absolutely anything in my life.

We all need friends and we have loved ones in whom we confide, but Giancarlo was the one person I could turn to about any issue.

There were times when I leaned on him for support and he was always there for me. When I was out for almost a year injured after joining Rangers, I spent a lot of time speaking with him.

When I was experiencing troubles in my personal life, I knew Giancarlo would listen and dispense advice. He just seemed instantly to know what kind of man I was.

We were not of a similar age, but neither was he an old man. He suffered a stroke last year when he was only in his early 60s and I would visit him whenever I returned to Italy.

But on my last trip to Florence, back in October when I was injured and allowed to return, I visited him but did not see him. He was asleep and I didn't want to disturb him.

I feel a guilty about that now because I returned to Glasgow and three or four days later, I received a call telling me Giancarlo had died.

He was a true friend and I will never forget him.

Knowing Giancarlo helped me settle down quite easily in my new surroundings and within six months I had bought my own flat because I felt at home there. I could not have asked for anything more off the pitch and on it we had big-name players like Francesco Toldo in goal, the Swede Stefan Schwarz in midfield and up front the brilliant Argentine striker Gabriel Batistuta. The Portuguese playmaker Rui Costa, who was to become one of my best friends, was also there at the time. We still speak on the phone to each other quite a lot and as well as being a wonderful footballer he is also a great guy.

I keep in touch with Michela Serena as well and obviously Bigica, who is more like a brother than a friend. We were born near each other and came through at Bari together before going to Florence. I am actually his son's Godfather and very proud to be so. We are very close and speak almost every day.

Batistuta is a guy I liked when I was at Fiorentina but I cannot say we are close friends. He is the kind of guy who I don't think believes in long-term friendships. When you are there he will talk to you and do anything for you. He will go to dinner with you and maybe go to a disco or something and you will have a good time but as soon as you go away he is not the type to phone you and keep in contact.

You have to phone him all the time if you are to keep things going and to be honest, I don't like that. If there is a friendship it has to be a two-way friendship. When we see each other we always greet each other as friends, asking how each of us is doing and things like that. I went to watch him when he played for Roma against Liverpool last year.

He is a good guy but maybe it is a South American trait because Gabriel Amato was exactly the same. Gaby and I were very close when he was at Rangers but as soon as he went away I didn't hear from him again. No phone calls, nothing! I can't do that. When I am very friendly with somebody it doesn't matter where in the world I am. Friendships are important to me. People think that if you are a footballer everything is always beautiful but, believe me, it is not. There can be very bad things as well.

We had a good team but we did not click immediately in my first season there. We were managing to win games but not with a lot of style. Gradually though, we started to settle down and after a couple of months we were playing very well. At Christmas we played AC Milan who were top of the table and we were second, just a point behind them. We drew 2-2 when we should have won it but going into the New Year we were still strong challengers.

More than that, we were progressing well in the Italian Cup and by that stage had got through four rounds. We were well up for it which is not always the case with some clubs and players in this competition.

But in the second half of the season we hit injury problems. I missed a few games with nothing serious, just knocks that were enough to keep me out, and Batistuta was the same.

We lost a few games and when the gap between AC Milan and ourselves stretched to seven points we knew we would not be bringing the title to Florence. We still finished second though, which was a fine effort, and although we had lost a few league matches we had managed to get through to the Italian Cup Final.

This was a huge thing for me because although I had various age-group international jerseys I had no silverware or medals to show for my professional career.

The Italian Cup Final is a two-legged affair and we were at home to Atalanta in the first game. It was a tight, tense affair in the rain with nobody willing to give their opponent an inch but Batistuta did what he does best and snatched us a goal after the Atalanta goalkeeper had made a mistake.

We hadn't played nearly as well as we could but we had a lead to take into the second game and that was the most important thing.

We knew it would be tough in Bergamo because it always is and Atalanta had finished the season playing great football.

But we wanted this badly and in the first half we played excellent football although we couldn't get the breakthrough and went in at the interval 0-0.

Just 10 minutes into the second half, however, we grabbed the vital goal. Sorry, I should say I scored the vital goal! I was up for a corner and normally it is my aerial ability that is used in those situations but this time the ball fell perfectly onto my right foot and I sent a great volley past their goalkeeper.

We all knew that going 2-0 up on aggregate meant the cup would be ours and when Atalanta threw men forward to try to get a goal back they left themselves open to the counter-attack and, inevitably, Batistuta took advantage to make it 2-0 on the night and 3-0 overall.

The scenes at the end were incredible. This was the first time in 26 years that Fiorentina had won a trophy so we all felt like history-makers.

We knew that a big celebration had been organised in Florence if we won the cup and all we wanted was to get back to our own people to join in the party. Unfortunately, we had a long wait.

The police kept us in the stadium for a full three hours after the match because there was a riot going on outside the stadium. The Atalanta fans were furious that their team had lost and they attacked the police and the Fiorentina fans who had been at the game.

Apparently it was mayhem outside and we couldn't get away until the streets had been cleared. Finally we got the all-clear and on the way to the airport we heard that 40,000 Fiorentina fans were waiting for us at our stadium.

The game had been live on big screens at our ground to enable the Fiorentina fans unable to get a ticket for the match in Bergamo to watch it together. The match had finished about 10.15pm and by the time our flight touched down in Florence and we made our way by bus to the stadium it was three o'clock in the morning – but it was like day-time. The floodlights were on full blast and the stadium was bouncing - nobody had left which was just unbelievable.

Walking onto that pitch to be greeted by them was one of the best feelings I've had in my life. It was an unforgettable night.

That was the good part of being a Fiorentina player. When the team did well, you were an idol.

But when the team did badly the idol changed to idiot in the eyes of the fans. They could make your life hell.

It happened to us the following season - my second in Florence. Like the first, we didn't start well but this time we didn't get ourselves out of the rut.

Batistuta could not score and when that wasn't happening the whole team was under pressure because he was our talisman. I think he ended up with 10 goals that season which is easily the poorest return he's ever had.

Toldo, who you may remember as the goalkeeper for the Italian team that reached the final of Euro 2000, had a terrible season as well. He lost unbelievably bad goals on a regular basis.

It didn't take the fans long to realise something was wrong but funnily enough we managed to reach the semi-final of the European Cup Winners' Cup where we were drawn against Barcelona.

The first leg was at the Nou Camp and it was a fantastic occasion for any player to be a part of. There were 110,000 of the most fanatical football fans in the world shoehorned into that magnificent old amphitheatre and the noise they made could probably be heard back in Florence.

But our fans back there would have been making plenty noise as well because we played superbly and came away with a 1-1 draw.

I had been handed the toughest job of my career before the game. I had to make sure Ronaldo didn't score. He was Barcelona's golden boy of course and the Brazilian was well on his way to becoming the world's greatest player. It was a massive task to try to stop him and for almost a month before the game I worked specifically on how I was going to counteract him.

I would stay behind after training and work with our head coach on how to make my feet quicker, how to enable me to turn more sharply and to be faster over five yards. We knew Ronaldo was greased lightning and someone who could make defenders look very silly and I was determined this was not going to happen to me.

The work paid off in the respect that over the two games Ronaldo did not score and I limited him to just one chance and that was in the first match in Barcelona. To this day I don't know how he got away from me. I was really tight on him, he had no room to move – and a split second later he was gone. Thankfully his shot missed the target but it was a sign that he had to be watched for every second of every minute.

He's the best striker I've come up against and at that time he was fully fit and flying. With respect to him, I don't think he is back at that level after all the injuries he's had. I know he had a great World Cup in Japan but for me he is about 80 percent of the player he was.

The Ronaldo I played against could turn and run away from any defender in the world. Now he can't. He is still a great player and I hope he can get back to his former glory but I don't know if it will happen.

We might have got a break when Ronaldo missed the one chance he got against us, but believe me that was the only piece of good fortune we had that night. We left Spain believing we had been robbed.

The referee chalked off what we thought was a perfectly good goal and he booked Batistuta for something innocuous which meant we were without our main striker for the second game because he had received a yellow card in a previous round.

But the ref saved his best for last. In the final minute Barcelona surged forward but I anticipated what they were trying to do and broke it up before sending our team forward on the counter attack.

We had three forwards against two defenders just outside the Barcelona box and looking odds on to score when we heard the shrill blast of the whistle to signal the end of the game.

We could not believe it. We surrounded the referee but he kept just tapping his watch saying it was time up. There was nothing we could do about it.

The return match was a huge disappointment. We know it would be tough without Batistuta but we made it even harder for ourselves after just 15 minutes when Toldo made another blunder.

We gave away a free kick out wide and when Sergio delivered it high into our box we expected Toldo, who is a big, big, guy, to come and collect it. Instead he stayed on his line and Fernando Couto was able to head Barcelona into the lead.

About 10 minutes after that I fouled Ronaldo just outside the box. Toldo lined up the wall but was then unsighted and Guardiola took advantage to score at the near post. It was another avoidable goal.

The referee was crazy. He denied Oliviera a penalty for us and booked him for his trouble and we went in at half-time knowing we were in trouble.

Desperate situations call for desperate measures and the manager said to me: "Lorenzo, we need someone up front to hold the ball up and to win things in the air - you will be the centre-forward in this half."

We needed three goals and it was always going to be tough, especially as I had not played up front since I was a kid in the Bari youth teams. I thought I did quite well and we created a few chances but it wasn't to be.

We got nothing from the referee who compounded his error of booking Oliviera in the first-half by red carding him after the break.

I don't remember the referee's name but I recall he was Swedish, the same as Stefan Schwarz, who was furious at him. I remember Stefan shouting at him: "You might be Swedish but I hope I never see you again."

The red card was the signal for the crowd to lose the plot. They started ripping up seats and throwing them onto the pitch. They tried to climb the fences to get onto the field and were beaten back by the police. It was bedlam and the referee was forced to take us off the pitch and back to our dressing rooms.

There were still 15 minutes left and eventually when some sort of order was restored we finished the match but we knew we were out. The club was banned from playing its next three home matches in Europe because of the incident. Barcelona went on to win the Cup Winners' Cup, beating Paris St Germain in the final, but for us the season was over because our league placing meant we could not qualify for the UEFA Cup and we were out of the Italian Cup.

We still had five or six games to play, however, and the fans weren't going to let us get away easily with having let them down so badly.

So they did something that I suppose British fans will think is hard to believe - they came to the dressing room to tell us face to face what they thought of us.

I don't know how many of them turned up - maybe a couple of dozen or so who were nominated as spokesmen for the rest - but their message was this: "We know you can lose but you need to lose in a good way. You need to fight, you need to work and you need to show the fans that you care because we pay your wages."

The players listened, mostly in silence, because some of the things they said were right, but no player goes onto the pitch wanting to lose. But it was worrying to be confronted by so many angry people. Every club has its share of crazy fans and Fiorentina is no different. But fortunately these guys didn't go too far.

We told them we still had a few games to go and we would give them everything we had and it worked out because we played better and won the last few matches. So maybe it was down to them storming the dressing room, I don't know.

Their passion for the club is astonishing. They follow them everywhere and 10,000 went to Barcelona for that match I spoke about earlier.

It is great for the players because they get a lift when they go to any stadium in the world and see that there are people there shouting and singing for them.

Little did I know that I would soon be swapping one set of the most fanatical supporters for another.

# *Chapter Four*

## BUTCHERED AND BEVVIED

YOU may have gathered by what I've already written that Italian football fans are not the most tolerant in the world. When things go great they are the best. When things go bad they are the worst.

The one thing above all they can't stand, however, is to hear that one of their players is leaving their team. Remember what happened to my friend Bigica in Bari?

No, these people treat a player's decision to leave as an act of betrayal. They see it as being left for another lover and their response can be irrational to say the least.

It is against this background that I will tell you how I first heard of Rangers' interest in me. Back in February of the season 1996/97 - the season it all went wrong for Fiorentina - I had heard whispers of interest in me from two English clubs, Leeds United and Blackburn Rovers.

To be honest, the thought of going to either of them failed to set my pulse racing. I was playing for Fiorentina in the best league in the world so why move to England?

Anyway, nothing came of those tentative inquiries and I thought nothing more about leaving Florence.

That is until one night in May when I took a phone call at the most inappropriate time in the worst possible place to be talking about leaving my club.

I was at a supporters' function near Florence when Andreas D'Amico, my agent, rang me on my mobile. He told me: "I have some interesting news. The Scottish club Glasgow Rangers are interested in talking to you."

Now at this exact moment I was surrounded by about 500 very excitable Fiorentina fans. This was not the best time to be talking to someone about leaving Florence, believe me!

"I can't talk about this right now, Andreas," I told him and said I would speak to him later. I was just about to switch off my mobile telephone when it rang again. This time it was Fiorentina's director of football speaking into my ear.

He said: "Rangers want you and they are willing to offer you and us a lot of money."

This was getting quite scary now. I kept looking around to make sure nobody could hear what was going on.

My first reaction was similar to the feelings I had when I heard that Leeds and Blackburn were interested in me. I shrugged my shoulders and thought: "I don't know much about Scotland. I don't know if I want to go there."

The next day I went to Fiorentina with Andreas to speak to

the directors, who made it clear that they were interested in accepting the offer Rangers had made for me. Then David Murray, the Rangers chairman, called as had been pre-arranged.

This was my first contact with Murray but he was to become a very important figure in my life and a man that I have come to admire greatly. I spoke some English at the time, but it was nowhere near as good as it is now. However even with my fractured English was able to pick up what he was saying and he was very persuasive.

Murray told me I would be joining the best team in Scotland. Rangers were the Juventus of his country, he claimed. The No.1 club and the aim was to keep them there and to make an impression in European competition. He told me about Ibrox and about the incredible passion the Rangers fans had for their club.

He emphasised how much he would be willing to pay me and even by Italian standards it was a good offer. Still, I swithered. I was only 26 and coming to the peak of my career. I was not sure I wanted to leave Italy at that stage in my life.

Also, niggling away at the back of my mind was a problem I had been having with my Achilles tendon. It had been worrying me on and off but I had been able to play through the problem although it had been concerning me enough to go to a top specialist in Antwerp, Belgium, Professor Maertens, just two days before Rangers made contact.

He told me I needed an operation but that it would not be necessary until the end of the season. I would have time to recuperate over the summer and be as good as new for the start of the following season.

That was playing on my mind a little but Mr Murray convinced me and my agent to come to Scotland for a look around.

Andreas shrugged as if to say: "It can't do any harm to have a look," so we arranged to travel to Glasgow. We booked via London and when we arrived at Heathrow and were waiting on our connecting flight to Glasgow, Andreas took a call on his mobile.

It was from Martin Edwards, the chief executive of Manchester United.

Andreas passed the phone and Edwards told me: "Listen Lorenzo, we know you are going up to talk to Rangers but don't do anything crazy. Don't sign anything when you are there because we want you to come here. We want to talk to you as well."

This had come out of the blue of course, and my head was spinning. I still had four years left of my contract in Florence and wasn't desperate to leave there. But now I was being given the choice to stay, or go to Scotland's biggest club or England's biggest club.

I know that many other people in that situation might have thought coming to Scotland was third in that list because, with respect, it is a fact that the league is not as strong as Serie A or the English Premiership.

But Rangers could give me a guarantee of European football, most often the Champions League, and that was a stage I wanted to sample. Nowadays, of course, four teams from Italy and England go into the Champions League but back then it was only the champions and runner-up, so it wasn't quite so definite that I would get that level of competition if I stayed in Florence or moved to Manchester.

United are a massive name of course and I would be lying if I said that they were not a huge temptation but I had given my word that I would travel to Glasgow so we boarded the flight and as soon as I arrived I realised I was in another massive football city.

The Press had taken over the airport and when I entered the arrivals hall they were all over me, asking me when I would be signing and what did I know about Scottish football.

I said to Andreas: "This is crazy - I haven't even said I would be signing for Rangers yet these guys are doing this!" I spoke to them in English a little bit but my mind was all over the place and I doubt if I made much sense.

Eventually I got out of the airport and was taken to Cameron House, a lovely hotel on the banks of Loch Lomond. If Rangers were trying to impress me by taking me to a place of such scenic beauty then it worked because it is a lovely setting.

After booking in I met the man who was to sign me, the Rangers manager Walter Smith. It was the day of the 1997 Champions League Final between Borussia Dortmund and Juventus and we all sat down to watch the game in the evening.

We had a good long chat with Walter, during which he told me how he saw me fitting into his team and what his plans were. I just kept thinking that I hadn't signed a contract yet but he was speaking to me as if I was already a Rangers player.

We spoke for a long, long time, which if you know Walter you will know is very possible because he is a lovely man. But I still hadn't decided that I would sign.

The next morning they asked me if I would go for a medical because they knew about the problem with the Achilles tendon. After looking at it they agreed that I needed an operation but like Professor Maertens, they didn't think it was a major problem.

By this time Andreas and I had heard from his office in Italy that Manchester United had faxed a contract outlining the deal they were willing to offer me. It seemed they were determined to get me and of course I was flattered but I was coming round to the idea that coming to Rangers might be the best thing for me to do.

My first sight of Ibrox Stadium only reinforced that feeling. As we drove towards that massive red-bricked frontage I was thinking: "This is a fortress." A look inside the stadium took my breath away even further.

I met the chairman for the first time that morning and I spoke with him about the deal and about the club. My agent told Mr Murray that we had received an offer from Manchester United that morning. Murray just smiled and said: "I know. I know they've sent you a fax. I know everything."

At the time I was surprised but it didn't take me long to realise that to be as successful in business as David Murray has been, you have to know everything!

I told him I wanted to go for lunch to think things over and I would give him a decision in the afternoon. At that point the big issue was really whether I wanted to leave Italy for Britain. Not whether I would choose Glasgow or Manchester as my home.

But I looked David Murray in the eye and made him a promise. I said: "If I decide to come to Britain, I will sign for Rangers."

It was almost a spur of the moment thing to say but I meant it. It was a gut instinct. I had met Walter, now I had met the chairman and somehow it all felt right.

It wasn't as if I was getting more money by going to Rangers. The Manchester United offer was almost identical so that didn't come into the equation. I also know that most people I spoke to in Italy believed I was crazy to reject a club like Manchester United but that didn't bother me. I've always been single-minded – some would say stubborn – so I wouldn't let popular opinion sway me.

It's difficult to explain why I took the decision. Always in my life I have followed my instinct. It is something inside me and I am a great believer in first impressions telling the truth. Walter had made a big impression on me and so had the chairman. My intuition was telling me that I could be happy here.

I went for lunch and hardly had time to eat because I spent much of the time on the phone. I wanted to speak to people who had travelled a bit. I knew the lifestyle I was leaving behind if I decided to move away from Florence. I would miss my family, my friends and of course, the weather.

But I didn't know what sort of place I would be coming to, so Andreas and I took a trip around Glasgow city centre after our meal and we liked what we saw. Lots of nice restaurants and good shopping. I was happy with that.

But Glasgow also played a trick on me that day. The sky was blue and the sun was warm!

A previous girlfriend of mine had studied English in Ireland for 18 months and one of her best friends is from Glasgow. I chatted with her and she told me that the people were very friendly and that were was a very strong Italian community in the city.

I was getting good vibes about the football club and now about the city and I decided that yes, I would sign for Rangers.

Throughout lunch I kept thinking about the impression Murray had made on me. I am an ambitious man and I always want to improve myself. I looked at Murray and I saw an ambitious man who clearly had made a success of his life in the most difficult of circumstances.

This is a man who lost both his legs in a car accident when he was very young, in his early 20s I believe. Yet he did not look for sympathy. He fought the problems that were put in his way – problems that we can't begin to understand – and he made his life a success.

To do what he has done shows incredible strength of character and I like and admire people like that.

He reiterated to me what he had said on the phone – that he wanted to make Rangers a power in Europe. He already had signed Jonas Thern for the following season and I was an admirer of the Swedish midfielder having played against him when he was at Roma.

Now Murray wanted me to be another vital part of the team and I was ready to go for it.

So after lunch and after the trip around Glasgow we went back to Ibrox to sign the contract.

The club moved very quickly and that very afternoon we had a press conference at the stadium with Walter and the chairman there to announce that I had signed. I shared the top table with Staale Stensaas, the Norwegian left-back who signed on the same day.

I knew I was coming to a big club but I think for Staale it was even more challenging because coming from a small league like Norway to a team like Rangers was a massive step and it was a pity that things didn't really work out for him at Ibrox and he has now returned to Rosenborg.

I really enjoyed that day to be honest. The Press conference was a weird experience because I could hardly understand a word of it. I was being asked all kinds of questions but I found the Scottish accent indecipherable.

I turned to Andreas and said: "What language are they talking? I thought they spoke English!"

Even Andreas, whose English was better than mine, was struggling. I sat there thinking I would have to take many lessons in Scottish English.

I remember Walter Smith being asked: "What do you think about this guy?" He thought about it for a minute before replying: "One thing is for sure... I am not going to give him my wife's telephone number!"

Everybody collapsed laughing except me because I could not understand what had been said but when it was translated to me I joined in and at that point I thought playing for Rangers was going to be a lot of fun.

Little did I know that before the fun there would be enough heartache and despair to have me questioning whether I would ever play football seriously again.

After the press conference I flew back to Italy in the chairman's plane. That was another impressive touch, I can tell you, then I told everyone in Italy I was moving abroad.

It caused quite a stir because at that time very few Italians left the country to play in another country. Pasquale Bruno had done it and he was having a good time in Scotland with Hearts. Paolo di Canio, of course, was at Celtic and Benito Carbone had gone to England.

As I said, most of the people back home told me I was nuts to go to Scotland and that annoyed me. I told them I wasn't an idiot and I'm not going to pretend I did it purely for the football. The fact is, I moved for the money.

Some players say that they move just for a change of scenery. To me, THAT'S crazy. I came to Britain because I was being offered a lot of money. For me the footballing choice came down to Glasgow or Manchester, but I left Italy because I was getting paid better in Britain and I don't feel the need to apologise for that fact.

It wasn't the only reason, though. I fancied the idea of living in another country, learning a different language and opening my mind to a different lifestyle.

So I signed the contract on the Thursday night and completed the deal that earned Fiorentina £4million.

The Achilles was still nagging away at me and when I arrived I spoke to the Rangers doctor at the time, Dr Cruickshanks, who told me that while the club was aware I had been dealing with

Professor Maertens, they wanted me to go to a clinic in London for the operation. I was a little bit upset because I trusted Maertens but I had joined this new club and I didn't want to create the impression I was a trouble-maker by insisting that I used my own man for the operation.

It was too soon to be rocking the boat but looking back, the decision to keep my mouth shut was one of the worst I've ever taken in my life.

So I went to this specialist in London on the Monday morning after I signed and had the operation on my Achilles tendon. As soon as I came round from the anaesthetic I felt that something was not right but they said I would be fine.

About three or four days later I went back to Italy to start my rehabilitation but it still wasn't right. I was running and jumping but there was still pain in my Achilles.

When I came back, I spoke at length with the Rangers physio Grant Downie and he told me to be patient. He said it might take a little bit longer than I first imagined because something had been removed from my tendon.

But you know yourself when something isn't right and although I trained and played practice matches with my new team-mates I knew something was amiss.

Walter had arranged a pre-season friendly against Everton at Goodison Park, which was to be my debut and I played for just over an hour before the pain became too unbearable. The problem began after half an hour or so but I tried to ignore it. It just became sharper and more agonising with every step I took and eventually I had to signal to the bench that I could not continue.

The morning after the match my ankle was swollen grotesquely and I knew there was something seriously wrong. After a week or so I went back down to London and the same guy who had operated the first time told me that I would have to go under the knife again but this time he said it was only a very minor problem which would not take long to clear.

He told me I would be great in a month but I thought he was talking rubbish because after an operation there is little or no chance of being fit to play again in 30 days.

Again, I kept my mouth shut. Again, it was a huge mistake on my part because I should have insisted that I go to Belgium to get the problem cured. But I was desperate to play for Rangers and although I didn't believe this specialist in London, I WANTED to believe he was right and I was wrong.

But 20 days, 25 days, a month after the second operation the ankle was worse. I couldn't even walk when I got up in the morning. I bought three or four pairs of shoes in bigger sizes than I normally wear because there was no way my left foot would fit inside the shoes I had.

I was feeling terrible and there was a panic growing inside me with every passing day that showed no sign of improvement. Eventually, after about six weeks, I went to Walter and told him that I had tried the Rangers way now I wanted to do my own thing to solve this injury.

Walter told me he had no problem with that but Dr Cruickshanks asked me to go back with him to London to see the man who had twice operated on me. I went along just to hear what he had to say but I was still determined to go to Belgium and see Professor Maertens.

The London guy met with us and what he had to say drove me over the edge. "Oh, you know...we have been trying something different on you."

My agent Andreas was with me that day and it was a good job he was because I lost it with the guy in that treatment room.

"You have been trying something different?" I shouted at him. "What are you talking about - I am a football player, not an accountant. I have to play with this ankle and you have been experimenting on me!

"You can f**k off - you are never getting near me again."

Dr Cruickshanks and Andreas were standing between this guy and me telling me to calm down but I was too angry and had endured too much pain to be cool, calm and collected over this.

The guy was unbelievable though. He told me he could do a third operation that would solve the problem. I told him where he could shove his third operation and I stormed out of that place.

The first call I made was to the Fiorentina doctor, Marcello Manzoli, to get Professor Maerten's number in Antwerp. He gave it to me and within days I had an appointment with him in Belgium.

Dr Cruickshanks came with me because he too was very concerned by this time and I think he got a fright when he saw how I reacted in London. But there would be no repeat of that scene in Antwerp because I trusted Maertens completely.

The professor took one look at the ankle and with a horrified expression on his face he said: "Lorenzo, what has happened here?"

Dr Cruickshanks and I explained everything that had happened so far and I had a scan and x-ray that afternoon.

Maertens initial reaction scared me, to be honest. The look on his face told me that something had gone badly wrong with the treatment I had received up until that point.

For the first time I began to think that maybe I would not come out the other end of this with my career intact. My mind was whirling with a thousand possibilities. Am I finished as a professional footballer? What will I do with myself? How can this be happening to me?

I could hardly walk, for God's sake. If I couldn't put one foot in front of the other without feeling pain how could I ever run or jump or kick a ball again?

Professor Maertens did his very best to allay my fears, however, and after a long, long chat with him he convinced me that I would be able to come back from this as good as new.

He explained that in the ankle there is a buffer full of liquid that allows the tendon to move without scratching against the bone. There was a difference in approach between the doctor in London and Professor Maertens. The Professor's approach required me to have bone cut away to allow more space between the tendon and the bone.

Because I had been training and playing between the first and second operations the tendon was damaged by the constant rubbing and scratching.

"It can be repaired," he told me. "Don't worry about that. But this isn't going to take two months any more.

"You will be out for five, six or seven months, depending on the time it takes to heal naturally after the next operation."

It's a good job I was sitting when he delivered the news. If I hadn't been I might have had another injury for him to deal with because I would probably have fallen.

SEVEN MONTHS? That simply did not bear thinking about but the words kept echoing in my mind like some unwanted mantra.

I simply had no choice, though. The alternative was to give up playing and there was no way I was going to do that at 26 years old.

So the following week I returned to Antwerp to have a piece of bone cut away from my achilles tendon and finally, at the third time of asking - but the first time with my own specialist - everything went great.

When I came round from surgery I remember Dr Cruickshanks saying to me: "Lorenzo, I have never seen anything like that and I have seen a lot of operations in my life. It was really complicated and hard to watch."

I stayed in that hospital for a week to recuperate because I was in a terrible amount of pain in the days that followed.

Eventually I was allowed to return to Scotland in a big plaster cast and using crutches to support me. I felt terrible - I had been brought here to help Rangers and I could hardly help myself.

It took me a month before I was able to throw away the sticks and it was a another month after that before the plaster could come off.

Rino Gattuso, Marco Negri and Sergio Porrini made up the Italian quarter with me at Ibrox at the time. We didn't know each other that well before my arrival, with Rino being more or less just a kid coming through and the others I knew only on a professional basis having played against them when Marco was at Perugia and Sergio at Juventus.

But it was good to have a few countrymen around me at a time when I was new to Scotland and suffering all the problems I had with my injury. To tell you the truth, I don't know how I would have coped without their support.

Not that I coped very well even with their care, attention and concern as you are about to find out.

Rino was brilliant with me. I was staying in a flat in Glasgow but it had too many stairs leading up to it and with my leg in plaster I couldn't cope so he offered to let me stay in his flat in the city centre which was much easier.

I was there for a month and the only worthwhile thing I could do was be everybody's chef! The Italian boys would come back together after training almost every day and I would have made them their lunch or their dinner. Jorg Albertz came along quite often as well as I remember.

I've always enjoyed cooking and I'm not bad at it but this was not what I had come to Scotland to do. And although the boys tried to cheer me up I was miserable all of the time.

Also, I was never ever tired. Maybe it was because after leading such a hectic life for so long I was suddenly in a position where I was getting no exercise and I was doing nothing to exhaust me.

I wasn't sleeping well and worse than that, because I had nothing to do all day I was eating and drinking far too much.

Normally I don't drink anything other than the occasional glass of wine. But I started drinking in that period and when I started I found it hard to stop. Anyone will tell you that drinking any kind of alcohol to excess is bad for you but I was drinking something that not only made my head hurt but turned me into a fat slob.

Not for me the usual bad things like whisky or vodka. No, I almost became addicted to Bailey's.

Most people like the creamy texture and the whisky taste but they will drink maybe just one or two glasses of it. That was never enough for me. Every day, I would sit on Rino's sofa while he was out training and I would drink glass after glass of Bailey's while watching the television with my brain in neutral.

I didn't know what I was doing but I did know that the taste was pleasant and the feeling it gave me numbed the pain and took me out of myself, so I kept drinking it. I also felt it would help me get the sleep I craved.

I don't know how much of it I was going through but it was plenty and it was almost every day. As a consequence, my weight rocketed. I put on a stone in a month, which for a professional athlete is a disgrace. I was disgusted with myself but it was a vicious circle. I was unhappy, so I drank. I drank, so I made myself even more unhappy.

I would be drunk when Rino and the guys would come in and

they would know I was but they found it difficult to say anything. So we would all have dinner and in the evenings it was better because at least I had someone to talk to.

Then the cycle would start all over again the following day and I knew I had to do something because I was slowly destroying myself. I looked in the mirror and didn't like what was staring back at me. Was this really me? Was I becoming an alcoholic? It was time to regain control of my life.

It was doing me no good being in Scotland at this time. I couldn't train or be of any use to anyone so I went to see Walter and asked him if I could return to Italy to be with my family and friends.

Walter agreed and we made arrangements that now and again Grant Downie the physio, Dr Cruickshanks or Archie Knox the assistant manager would come out to see how I was getting along.

So I went back home at the end of September and I have to say that the people at Fiorentina were absolutely marvellous at this time. When I was able to start rehabilitation they allowed me to go to their physio and although it was difficult I made good progress.

I had to return to Italy, I have no doubt about that. I wasn't classified as being depressed in Scotland but I think I was. Not by the country but by the nightmare situation I found myself in. I had to get out. Had to break the vicious circle.

As soon as I arrived home I stopped drinking and made a determined effort to eat properly again. Things had to change - immediately - because I looked terrible.

The weather, inevitably, was better and I began to feel better about myself as well. Gradually, I was able to walk. My family came to Florence to be with me and I started to see Cristina my ex-girlfriend again and we started to make our relationship more serious.

I had already met her before I signed for Rangers but when I went to Scotland all we had were phone calls to each other.

Everything was getting better and the ankle was responding to the work with the physio.

By the middle of February, almost six months after that game against Everton, I was ready to return to Scotland and show the people that Rangers had not paid £4m for some injury-prone jinx from Italy.

I started training with the team and after a couple of weeks we had a game against Hearts coming up. Walter came up to me at the training session the day before the match and asked if I thought I was ready for it.

I wasn't sure. I'd had just one game with the reserves under my belt at that time and after being out for so long I was not convinced I was ready.

But we agreed that just to ease myself in, I would sit on the bench. I was pleased because my first-team return was so near.

Or so I thought.

During the training session we were doing an exercise and maybe I was sub-consciously compensating too much for the left ankle by putting too much pressure on the right one.

I remember reaching for a ball and my right ankle - not the one that had given so much grief - just made a noise that sounded like a cork being pulled from a bottle.

The Swedish defender Jocky Bjorklund was standing next to me as I fell to the ground howling and I remember him shouting: "What the f*** was that noise?" He was panicking and I was screaming: "I think I've broken my ankle." It was a nightmare beyond my comprehension having already been out for so long.

I was lying there on that training ground crying my eyes out. Not only because of the excruciating pain in my right ankle but because this was so unfair. I had worked so hard, exorcised so many demons, and now this.

We didn't have Murray Park at that time of course, but how I wish we had. That facility, near my home in Bearsden on the outskirts of Glasgow, has state of the art medical facilities within 50 yards of the training pitches.

But back then Rangers were training at various locations and we had to meet at Ibrox, get on a coach and travel to wherever we had been booked to train that morning. It was not an ideal situation for a club of Rangers' stature and I am glad that David Murray agreed to pay for the complex that was built last season.

So, I was helped into our coach John Brown's car and he had to drive me back to Ibrox where the damage on my ankle could be assessed by the doctor and physio. It was the longest journey of my life and not because Bomber is a maniac behind the wheel. He might be in every other way, but he drove very considerately that day!

I was still crying as we made our way back. Bomber was trying his best to console me, telling me everything would be all right and things like that. I phoned my brother Davide, who had come over to Scotland to be with me for a little while I settled into this country all over again, and he rushed over to Ibrox as well.

When he saw me crying he started to cry as well. Who said Italians were emotional people? But we were both in despair at the time and it was only when I was taken to the hospital and tests showed that nothing was broken that I was able to calm down.

The doctors told me I had been lucky. I had suffered a very bad twist but there was no lasting damage.

But the incident cost me another month on the sidelines, which at the time seemed like an eternity.

The frustration is impossible to describe actually. I was fit, I was ready to sit on the bench and then...nothing for another month. It was a never-ending nightmare to be honest but there was nothing I could do except be strong and be determined that when this injury healed nothing was going to stop me being a success for Rangers.

I don't think anyone can really understand what it is like for a player to be out for so long unless he has gone through it himself. That's why I have such sympathy for boys like Michael Ball and Michael Mols at Rangers who have had such wretched luck with long-term injuries.

I have spent a lot of time speaking with them, trying to encourage them and telling them that if I can come back then so can they. But ultimately, only they can deal with their problems and it is soul-destroying to keep coming back then finding another hurdle that has to be overcome.

But the doctors called it correctly when they said this ankle injury would take a month to clear. It did, and the timing co-incided with one of the biggest weeks of the season for Rangers.

We were going for ten-in-a-row in what we knew by this time would be Walter Smith's last season as manager of Rangers. He had announced his intention to stand down back in November at the club's annual general meeting, a decision which disappointed me greatly as my injury had meant that I hardly got to work with a man I admire so much.

I was actually back in Glasgow for a few days just to see everyone at the club when he made his announcement and I know it was a difficult time for him.

I pulled him aside one morning and asked him why he was leaving. He simply said: "When your time is up, it is up." I think he believed that having won nine-in-a-row his team was on the verge of breaking up and when all his boys were leaving he felt he should go with them.

Anyway, the hype was unbelievable because winning 10 championships in a row was something that had never been achieved in Scottish football - or anywhere else I believe - and Celtic were giving Rangers a real run for our money this time.

We were due to play them twice in a week at around the time I was ready for selection. First up was a Scottish Cup semi-final, to be played at Celtic's ground because the national stadium at Hampden was undergoing renovation.

Although the game was to be played at Parkhead it was officially a neutral venue so the crowd was split 50/50, so it was half-filled with Rangers fans which was great. Since then, of course, I've played many times at Celtic Park and I've always been amazed at how the small number of our fans they let in - maybe 3000 - make so much noise.

But this day was different. We had half the stadium, so did they and the scene was set for one almighty battle.

I didn't really think I would be involved to be honest, because I had been out for so long and a match against Celtic is not one to take risks with.

But I went with the team to St Andrews to prepare and Walter said we'll see how things go in the days running up to the match. It turned out I did great in training and felt the confidence flooding back. I think adrenaline was getting me through because I knew that, finally, I was ready to play again.

The day before the game Walter told me I was on the bench. I thought it was a big decision for him to make but he told me that if I played as I had done in training I could handle it no problem.

I took my place on the bench that afternoon thinking that I would have time to study the flow and rhythm of the game and if necessary I might get the last 20 minutes or so. It was bedlam. Everyone had told me about these games but nothing can prepare you for the reality.

These two sets of fans are crazy and when you mix them together in the one stadium it is explosive. Their passion - and let's not kid ourselves - their hatred for each other transmits itself onto the pitch and the game is played at a frenzied pace. I had never seen anything like it in my life and I had been involved in some pretty high-tempo matches in Italy.

Anyway, I had time to get used it, I thought, as I settled back on the bench.

As usual I could not have been more wrong.

Only 19 minutes had passed when our big Yugoslavian defender Gordan Petric signalled to the bench that he had pulled his hamstring.

Walter looked at me and smiled. I could not believe he could smile amid all that tension, but he did. He said: "Lorenzo, it's your time."

Imagine how I felt at that moment. Out for 10 months. Never played a first-team game for Rangers. With hardly any training. And now I had to play for 71 minutes against Celtic in a game that meant everything to the people.

I hardly had time to get nervous but as I made the few steps from the dug-out to the centre line, to have my studs checked by the linesman, the Rangers fans blew away any apprehension I might have felt.

Every one of them was standing with their hands above their hands applauding me as I made my onto the pitch. If the Celtic fans were not giving me such a warm welcome to Scottish football, I didn't notice. It was the best feeling I have ever had going onto a football pitch.

I was back. It was a huge match. And these people who had waited so long to see me had not forgotten me. It was a wonderful moment for me and I went onto play excellently, if you will forgive me saying so myself.

We won 2-1 and the fans went crazy. I did as well, because this was a very significant moment in my career.

It proved so many things to me. I knew if I could come through a test like that one, that I was truly back as far as my ankle was concerned.

The following week, as luck would have it, we played Celtic again. This time in the league at Ibrox and we won 2-0. Two Old Firm matches in seven days and two victories. For Rangers fans it doesn't get any better than that.

Everything was going well and it was still very close in the race for the title but one dreadful afternoon in Aberdeen tilted the odds in favour of Celtic.

We lost the game and to make matters worse I was sent off by Willie Young. To this day I don't understand why he showed me the red card. We had won a free kick just outside Aberdeen's penalty box and there was the usual jostling as the wall was being lined up.

I was waiting to take the shot when an Aberdeen player came to stand over the ball. I shoved him out of the way, nothing more, and there was nothing malicious in it. We were losing the game 1-0 and I was wanting to get on with things.

But Willie ran over and flashed the red card in my face. I could not believe it and neither could my team-mates. I don't think even the Aberdeen players could believe it.

There were just 15 minutes left and we were pushing for the equaliser at the time but after the sending off we could not make the breakthrough so we lost the game and with it the leadership of the table which we had held going up to Pittodrie.

I missed the next game through suspension, against Hearts at Tynecastle, and although we won so did Celtic and they held a three point lead with two games left.

I returned for the penultimate game of the season against

Kilmarnock at Ibrox. We knew we had to win in order to put some pressure on Celtic who were away to Dunfermline the following day.

But it all went horribly wrong for us. We were nervous right from the start and we could not string three passes together. The pressure had got to us and we gave probably our worst performance of the season.

We created some chances and took none of them. Then as we pushed forward in the dying minutes Kilmarnock sprung out of defence and hit us with the classic sucker punch. There was no time to come back and as we came off the field we believed our chance was gone.

If Celtic won at Dunfermline the next day, the 10-in-a-row dream was dead and our dressing room was a desolate place that afternoon. Some of the boys who had been there a long time were crying but I felt estranged from the emotion they were displaying.

Most of them knew they were going at the end of the season and that an era in the club's history was about to end. Ally McCoist, Richard Gough, Andy Goram, Brian Laudrup, Ian Durrant, Stuart McCall - all great guys who had been through everything together and who wanted nothing more than to go out with another title.

Those boys were more than a team. They were like a family and it is something I had never known before in football or have known since.

They were entitled to cry but I was just here and my only tears would have been of frustration that I was unable to help them achieve their dream because of the length of time I had spent injured.

Funnily enough, Celtic didn't beat Dunfermline the next day. They drew 1-1 which meant we still had a chance on the final day. But we had to beat Dundee United at

Tannadice and hope St Johnstone beat Celtic at Parkhead.

We were confident we could do our bit but we knew it would be a miracle if Celtic didn't win in front of their own supporters that afternoon.

Sure enough, we won 2-1 but Celtic won their match 2-0 and for the first time in 10 years the championship trophy was not going to be displayed at Ibrox.

By the time we got into the dressing room at Tannadice we knew it was over. Nobody said a word until Archie Knox, in a quiet voice which was unusual for him because he is a larger than life character, said: "Don't worry Lorenzo, you will be here next year and for a lot longer than that. You will lift plenty of trophies for Rangers."

It was a great thing for me to hear because it showed that Archie and Walter didn't blame me for what had happened. Yet I blamed myself in part although I knew there was nothing I could do about the length of time I was out injured. The guilt was there though because I felt I had not made a big contribution to my first season in Scotland.

Walter had spent a lot of money on me and had been counting on me to play for Rangers and bring a different style to the team but I spent most of the time on operating tables or crutches and for me that was not good enough.

The league was lost but we still had the Scottish Cup Final to play and the majority of the team knew that it would be the last game they would play for the club. The desperation to win was so intense that you could almost smell it but we lost that game to Hearts at Celtic Park as well and the season ended barren in terms of silverware.

My friend Willie Young played a major part in this game as well. He awarded Hearts a penalty after just three or four minutes when Sergio Porrini pulled down Steve Fulton. It was clearly outside the box and everyone knew that without television cameras proving it afterwards but Mr Young pointed to the spot and we were 1-0 down before anyone had broken sweat.

We chased the game after that and came close a couple of times but a long ball out of the Hearts defence in the second half produced a slight misunderstanding between Richard Gough and me. Stephane Adam took full advantage, slipping in between us to add a second goal for Hearts.

It was a long way back for us now but we dug deep and with about 15 minutes to go Coisty came off the bench to get one back for us. We pushed forward with renewed belief, thinking that if we got a second goal we could win the match in extra time.

Coisty was giving everything. He knew this was his last match in a Rangers jersey and the born winner in him was shining through. He was fouled from behind inside the box in the closing minutes. It was a penalty. I knew it, Coisty knew it and even the Hearts players knew it.

But the one man who didn't know it was the man who mattered. Willie Young gave a free-kick on the edge of the box. We were furious but we were also helpless. We couldn't force him to change his mind and Hearts hung on to win their first trophy in many, many years.

It was the very end for Walter's team and we all knew how ironic it was that a decade of almost unbroken success should finish with nothing. The Rangers fans were magnificent. We had just lost a cup final but they wouldn't let this team walk away without showing their appreciation and it was too much for many of the boys.

We got back to the dressing room and a river of tears was released. Coisty was inconsolable. He was sobbing and he wasn't the only one. It was a terrible moment and if I needed a reminder of what this club means to people I got it in that dressing room that afternoon.

Apart from the crying, there was silence in our dressing room but we could hear the Hearts players celebrating wildly in theirs. That was perfectly understandable, of course. They had won the cup and it meant everything to them so they were entitled to sing and dance. But their joy contrasted sharply with the misery we were feeling and to be honest we couldn't get out quick enough to leave them to it.

We had arranged to go back to Ibrox for a big dinner with our families whether we won or lost the match and I learned something else very important that night.

We had won nothing but that night everybody enjoyed themselves. Of course, it was sombre at the start. Nobody felt like celebrating anything but gradually, the boys started talking about the great times they'd had. The matches they'd won, the trophies they'd lifted.

By the end of it, the players and the manager were drinking, dancing, smiling and hugging each other. I remember Stuart McCall saying to me: "Lorenzo, something very special is ending here, but really it will never end. We will always be bonded together no matter where we all end up playing."

And I joined in. I had only known this team a short while but it was enough to become part of them in a small way.

But in the back of my mind I was thinking: "I've won nothing with Rangers."

I hate losing. I always have and that night I promised myself that there would be no repeat the following season.

# *Chapter Five*

## BEATING THE BIGOTS

WHEN I came to Glasgow I knew a little bit about the religious divide that separates Rangers from Celtic. But, if I am being truthful, I have to admit I didn't realise how deep-rooted it was, certainly as far as the supporters of both clubs are concerned.

Paolo di Canio tried his best to explain it to me the first time I came to Glasgow. I met him in the Il Pavone restaurant in Princes Square and even that would have seemed wrong to some people. After all, Paolo was a Celtic player and I was about to become a Rangers player, so in their eyes I should hate him.

That is rubbish, of course. Paolo and I are friends and no

matter which teams we played for that would never change.

Paolo told me I was joining a massive club but he warned me to be very careful. He said: "Don't forget you are a Catholic and a lot of Rangers fans don't like Catholics. You will have to prove yourself to them even more than usual because they will see you as a Catholic first and a football player second."

With hindsight I have to disagree with Paolo because the welcome the Rangers fans gave me, especially in my debut against Celtic, is something that will live with me forever.

But he was giving me advice as a friend and at the time I appreciated his concern for me.

It turned out, though, that the biggest problems I had in Glasgow came not from the Protestants who support Rangers but the Catholics who follow Celtic. Obviously not all of them, but some of them clearly believe I did a terrible thing by joining a club that for most of its history refused to sign a Catholic player.

I had not even been at Ibrox a week when I received a letter, anonymously written, marked for the attention of myself, Rino Gattuso, Marco Negri and Sergio Porrini - the four Italians at Rangers.

It told us that we had chosen the wrong team and that we had betrayed our religion by joining Rangers. It called us mercenaries who had put money before our faith and it questioned how we could play for a club whose fans sing songs against The Pope and against Catholic people.

The letter told us to cancel our contracts immediately. It even said that if we wanted to play in Scotland we should sign for Celtic! Now, even though I had only been in Scotland for a few days I knew that anyone suggesting that a player leave Rangers to join Celtic, or the other way round, has to be crazy.

Near the end of the letter its tone turned more sinister. It seemed to suggest that we would find it very difficult to live in

Glasgow having made this decision to play for Rangers.

It said: "I feel sorry for the four of you. If something happens to you, don't blame us because you have brought this problem upon yourselves. Take care because from now on, anything can happen to you."

I took that as a threat and I don't mind admitting I was concerned. I spoke better English than the other three Italian guys and I tried to explain the content of the letter and they were also worried.

I spoke to Walter Smith and he tried to ease our fears by saying there were a lot of stupid people out there and we would probably get a few letters like this, but that nothing would happen. He said the vast majority of the people here were decent and sensible and would realise that we were all just doing our job.

He advised us to throw the letter in the bin and he promised that if the threats kept coming he would take action by going to the police or whatever. Thankfully he was proved right and nothing came of it.

But the incident opened my eyes to the fact that I had wandered into a minefield. Not only were the Rangers fans going to look at me with suspicion. It seemed the Celtic supporters would harbour a grudge simply because I am a Catholic who chose to earn my living playing for Rangers. It is crazy and it is stupid but it is there and even now they boo me whenever I play in an Old Firm game.

Even when I go into the city I occasionally get stick from Celtic fans. They call me a traitor and sometimes it gets worse than that. I've been out at night and been hassled by people who think they can make a name for themselves by having a go at Lorenzo Amoruso.

But I don't encourage them in the slightest. For me, the strongest man is the man who walks away from the provocation these idiots attempt. I don't have to show my power or my strength. I know I have it so why give them the satisfaction of seeing me lose the plot with them? I would not be drunk but they would be - they would have to be to say some of the things that are said. And a drunk man can be unpredictable. If I say something back he might have a bottle or a knife.

These people might not have much to lose but I have everything to lose if I allow them to get to me, so I don't.

But I am not stupid enough to think that it doesn't happen on the other side as well. I am sure Rangers fans sometimes have a go at Celtic players when they are on nights out and that is very sad as well. I know that Neil Lennon has had problems and he has to learn to walk away because before you know it, these things are all over the papers and you get a reputation you don't deserve.

I really feel sorry for him because of all the trouble in Ireland. I know that threats have been made against him and his family and that is the worst thing that can happen to a person.

If people don't like me, they can shout at me. But the abuse should never involve a person's family. That is stepping over the line and that is why I have so much sympathy for Lennon. The public have to realise we are just normal guys who love our job and try to do our best on the pitch.

All we ask is that people just let us play. We are not robots or extra-terrestrials. We are just people trying to live our lives.

There is nothing sensational about a Catholic - from any country including Scotland - playing at Ibrox.

I don't know what all my team-mates beliefs are but I do know I believe in something. I am a Catholic and I believe in Jesus Christ but that doesn't make me a better player or a worse player.

I signed a contract with Rangers and I gave them my word I would give them 100 percent for as long as they paid my wages.

For as long as I am here, I will give everything of myself to this club. Never mind my religion. It has nothing to do with this.

I have to thank the Rangers fans, though. They might have had doubts in the beginning but they did not transmit them to me. They could have complained when I was made captain because I don't think there had been a Catholic skipper before, but by that time I think they knew that I was the type of player who gave his heart and soul to the club and wanted to make it better.

To be honest, I don't get too much grief any more but maybe that's because I don't go out at night in Glasgow very often. When I do, as I said, I keep a clear head so that I always have my wits about me.

If I want to drink I stay at home and have a bottle or two of wine with some friends. That keeps me away from trouble.

But the religious situation in Glasgow does sadden me. Religion has been the basis of so many wars over the centuries but people here have welded it onto football and I can't understand that. Don't forget we are playing a game here, that's all. It is not about whether Catholics are better people than Protestants or vice versa. It is not life or death, no matter how important it might seem during the 90 minutes.

I am not going to say it is pleasant for an Italian to hear Rangers fans singing F**k The Pope. Of course it's not. I have my beliefs and they have theirs but during a game I don't let it get to me because I am focused fully on doing my job. It is a background noise, if you like, and I ignore it. I know what they sing is stupid but I also know that the bad things they sing about Catholics is not the truth, so why should I let it bother me? I can't get involved in it and I don't. If Catholic people think that makes me a traitor, then too bad. I know within myself I am a good person, so it doesn't matter what they say or think.

Of course, I would love Rangers fans to stop singing sectarian songs but I don't think they will. But for as long as they sing them I will continue to let the noise pass through one ear and out the other.

I don't think they really think too hard about what they are singing either. I mean, the Rangers fans like me and I like them, so they are not singing these things to upset me. I think they do it because they know it annoys the Celtic fans, just as the fans of that club sing about the IRA and stuff like that to provoke a reaction from the Rangers support.

When I first came here, several people including Walter Smith advised me not to cross myself as I ran onto the pitch because it would antagonise the Rangers fans. I know a lot of Italians in Glasgow and most of them are Celtic supporters but they also told me not to make the sign of the cross in front of the Rangers crowd. I thought that was ridiculous because whether or not I cross myself does not mean I will run faster or tackle harder, but I was in a strange land so I complied. I know, of course, Walter and the others were telling me this to protect me more than anything else. They didn't want me getting off on the wrong foot here, so they were looking after me.

I still cross myself, of course. I just don't do it on the pitch. And for me it is as much a superstitious thing as a symbol of my religious faith.

The bottom line is that Rangers fans know I am Catholic but they also know I really love the club.

I hope that the religious situation in Scotland settles down as the years go on but maybe that is naivety on my part.

We are here to play football, not make political or religious statements, and hopefully the people can understand that and support us for what we do on the pitch, not because we go to this church or that church. Going to watch football should be a joyful experience. To go there specifically to sing about killing

Protestants or Catholics seems crazy to me.

I have read in the newspapers or seen on the television the stories of fans of both sides being killed in fights after Rangers-Celtic games. I am only a small voice but I would ask everyone to think about this. Is it really worth it?

I am sure the people who have done these terrible things will regret it for the rest of their lives but that is nothing compared to the families and friends who have lost loved ones simply because they were wearing a blue or a green scarf in the wrong place at the wrong time.

There is nothing else really to say on the subject. It is completely stupid and there is nothing I would like more than for the hatred to stop.

The religious situation is just one of the pressures that comes with playing for the biggest club in this football-crazy country and like everyone else I need time and space to unwind now and again.

For me that means getting away from it all and indulging in some hobbies that give me a sense of freedom and a great deal of enjoyment.

One of them has brought a little bit of criticism from some quarters. There are some people who are very much opposed to anyone who hunts wildlife and when I once told a newspaper that one of my favourite past-times is going to into the Perthshire countryside to shoot, there were some people who wanted me to stop.

It was not a big issue - there were no threats from animal rights groups or anything like that - but I read that some people were saying that someone with a high-profile like I have should not be publicising this kind of thing.

I think that's nonsense and hopefully I can explain why.

I first started shooting when I was in Italy but, to be honest, it is only since I came to Scotland that it has become something of a passion in my life.

Over in Italy I have my friends and my family and I have a busier social life. Also, when I played there, we tended to train in the afternoon which meant that by the time you got out of your bed and had your breakfast, it was time to go to your club. In other words, there wasn't a lot of spare time.

In Scotland we train in the morning which means that most afternoons there a few hours to spare. I have my close circle of friends here, of course, but generally there is more free time for me to indulge in my hobbies.

My friend Vito organises shooting and hunting days in Perthshire and he invited me up for the first time at a period when I was very low. It was at the time when the supporters were being very critical of me and after one home game against Dundee United they had booed me and I was very upset.

Vito, being a very good friend, knew I had to get away from it all for a day just to clear my head and think about something else other than football, so he persuaded me to join him in the Perthshire hills for a day's shooting.

My first victim was a pigeon - but keep your hair on, it was a clay pigeon!

I really enjoyed that, just banging away at the flying targets. It was a great way of getting rid of the stress I was under at the time and for the few months that's all I shot.

Eventually, Vito asked me if I fancied trying to shoot game and I started with ducks, pheasants, partridges, that kind of thing.

Now before I go any further, I want to make this clear. Lorenzo is not some kind of savage who will do this for fun then just leave the body of the dead animal or bird lying in the countryside.

I eat everything I shoot. I clean it up and I bring it home either to cook in my house or I take it to a couple of my favourite restaurants and they prepare it for me and my friends.

After about a year, I was asked if I would like to try shooting wild deer. This was a much bigger challenge but I thought I would give it a try.

I didn't know if I could do it and to be fair Vito doesn't like doing it. Maybe he has watched the film Bambi too many times, I don't know.

My first time was a disaster. For a start, I was using a rifle which I had been practising with and doing fine. But that was when I was training the sights on stationary targets.

The reality was very different. The guy I was with took me to this secluded valley and we saw four or five wild deer roaming around. We were hidden - they couldn't see or smell us and it was perfect. My guide told me: "Just relax, concentrate, and squeeze the trigger."

I did it and I missed. The shot rang out making a huge noise but the deer didn't run away. They looked around but because we were in a valley, there was an echo and they didn't know where the shot had come from.

So I thought: "That's okay, I'll get one the next time." So I squeezed the trigger again. Bang. Nothing fell to the ground. The deer continued to look around, but not in a panicky way. It's as if they were thinking: "Nothing to worry about here - it's a blind man shooting at us."

I tried again. Third time lucky I thought. But no, I failed again and eventually the deer got fed up with it and wandered up a hill.

I was laughing by this time because it was ridiculous.

We decided to come back at night with a spotlight and hunt some more deer. This time I hit one first time. It went down and it was a clean kill. The animal did not suffer.

The guide opened the deer up to take out the internal organs and when he had its liver in his hands, he dragged it across my face. He explained that it was tradition to mark the killing of your first deer in this way.

The animal was cut up and I took the meat home with me. As I said, I would never kill an animal just for the fun of it. I don't like to see people making a sport of it and hanging the heads of deer on their walls like some kind of trophy.

If anyone complains about me hunting, and as I said, I haven't had a lot of hassle over it, I just say that I don't see the difference between eating a deer and eating a cow. If they say it is cruel to kill it, I say that every steak or every chicken that everyone eats has been killed at some point.

There are animals and birds which are born purely to be eaten by man. They are kept in terrible conditions until they are big enough to be killed. That, for me, is much more inhumane than hunting a wild animal that has had a good life roaming the beautiful Scottish countryside.

And it tastes better. Wildlife has no fat and you can taste the difference. I make no apology for my shooting.

Fishing is something else I do occasionally but not with a rod. I've tried fly-fishing and didn't like it. I couldn't really get the hang of it.

I much prefer to fish underwater with a spear-gun and I do that in the summer back in Italy. I do that with my friends when I go home, both in the day, and at night with a underwater torch. It's great fun.

Night-time is the best because there are not so many people in the water and the fish are not as alert as they are during the day.

It is a great relaxation because when you are under the water you have entered another world completely. You feel very small and insignificant down there because the sea has all the power and you are nothing in comparison to it.

It is much more dangerous than shooting. The moment you think you are in charge of the sea is the moment you are in trouble. As I wrote earlier, I lost a very good friend of mine to the sea. He was an expert diver and his death taught me to always have complete respect for the sea. It is always the boss.

Other hobbies? Well, living in Scotland I had to learn to play golf and I must admit I love it.

I was getting quite good at it until last year when I had a bad shoulder injury and I had to stop playing golf for seven or eight months.

When I re-started I found, as everyone does, that it takes a long time to get your game back to the level it was at. But I'm getting there slowly. When the weather is good and you are out there on some of the finest courses, there really is nothing like it. Unfortunately, the weather is not always good...

I basically enjoy anything that takes my mind off football when I am not training or playing. It might seem odd to some people but I don't immerse myself in the game. Football has been my life for as long as I can remember and it is important for me that I can switch off from it when I have some spare time.

I don't watch a lot of it on television, for instance. I don't have Sky TV although I have a satellite dish that allows me to watch Italian programmes and of course football is on that a lot.

It's the same with my friends. Most of them have no connection with football and that is important for me because we can speak about everything, not just about who is top of the league or who is playing great or playing badly.

Cooking is another leisure activity that takes my mind off football. I love preparing meals and you can lose yourself for a long time in the kitchen, working out menus and how to best prepare the meal. I like to think I am quite good and so far nobody has keeled over with food poisoning, so I must be doing something right.

I also read a lot, but not in the house funnily enough. When I travel I always have my nose stuck in a book but I can't do it at home and I don't know why.

I'm a big fan of Wilbur Smith - I love his novels. All of his books are about Africa and he gives a fantastic insight into this wild continent and the nature that exists within it. It fascinates me. I think it appeals to me because, as I have explained, I love to go into the countryside myself. Smith speaks about these things but in a much grander scale.

Talking of the countryside, I don't only go there to shoot. I also pick mushrooms. Some people here might think that's a strange hobby but a lot of Italian people roam the countryside looking for mushrooms.

I started doing it years ago when I would go out with my dad on Sunday mornings. He would have the day off and we would walk for miles just looking and collecting all kinds of mushrooms.

Even back then, I loved the sense of space and the fresh air. It was so different from the city.

When I came here I didn't think there would be much opportunity for mushroom picking. In fact I didn't think the Scottish weather would be right for growing them but I was wrong about that.

The first time I went shooting in Perthshire I was with a few people including Rino Gattuso's father and mother and we discovered plenty of mushrooms, so I have gone picking many times since then.

I think it's an Italian thing really. Most people from elsewhere don't feel comfortable doing it and I think that's because they don't know what they are looking for. They don't trust themselves because some mushrooms can be poisonous and they are scared of picking the wrong ones.

There are books which identify the right ones and the wrong ones but I don't need them now. I have been picking them long enough to know which ones can and can't be eaten.

It really is a relaxing, peaceful past-time. I love taking myself away to Perthshire and to Lanarkshire, actually, where there are some wonderful places that mushrooms grow. You will forgive me if I am not more specific about the locations...I want to keep them to myself!

These are things that keep me sane away from the game. Most of them though are dependent on the Scottish weather. I don't mind the cold - you can just put on a big coat and you are fine - but when it rains hard and the wind blows, that's another story.

# *Chapter Six*

## GETTING PLASTERED WITH GAZZA

FROM day one at Rangers I knew my life would never be the same again. Believe me, neither would yours if they gave you the seat next to Paul Gascoigne.

I had Gazza on my right and Richard Gough on my left. Talk about keeping bad company.

Gazza is a one off - a great guy - and he and I quickly became good friends. We hit it off straight away because he started talking to me in Italian. The only problem was almost every single word was a swear word.

He is a really funny boy and a great player - the kind of guy who even if you put him in an empty dressing room can make the atmosphere.

At that time - with the team going for 10 in a row - the atmosphere in the dressing room was unbelievable and Gascoigne was at the middle of everything.

Everybody who has played with him or got to know the guy will have a memorable Paul Gascoigne story - some good, some bad and some mad.

I always remember the day he turned up with an injured ankle and he was told to go to the treatment room to get it put in plaster.

The physio was working on it for ages making sure everything was just perfect because Gazza was such an important player.

At the end of the job he turned to Gazza and said: "Right, how does that feel?"

Gazza looked up and said: "That's fantastic, you've done a great job. There's just one thing ... it's the other ankle I twisted!"

But that's Gazza. Every day there was a new joke. It's just that some were funnier than others.

Gazza had some problems that season because, as I said in the previous chapter, the team was trying and failing to win ten successive league titles.

For most of the season I was looking in from the outside because I was injured for so long but I could see there was pressure on these guys and I could see also that different personalities had different ways of dealing with it.

For many of them the best escape was alcohol. Don't get me wrong, I'm not criticising any of them because sometimes everyone needs to relax and to clear their mind of stress and trying to make history was taking a heavy toll on this team.

And anyway, a lot of these nights were designed to build the camaraderie between the players.

I must admit I found it all a bit strange at first because in Italy everything is very different.

But I wanted to learn about the culture - even the drinking.

Back home of course, the players like a night out but these nights were few and far between. This was a different world.

But these were professional players all right and none more so than Goughie - and yet he was the very guy who would arrange the famous drinking sessions. So you will understand why I found it hard to get my head around it all.

Goughie took me through what Rangers Football Club meant. It was a great thing for me to learn what it meant to play for this team and Richard was the ultimate ambassador for the club. He breathed it.

I am still very good friends with him and speak with him quite a lot. It was he, Coisty and Durrant who made me feel part of the club when I joined.

If I thought things would be just the same as they'd been for me in Italy I was wrong. But one of the reasons I made such a huge change to my life when I left my country was to sample the way things were done elsewhere.

And believe me – things are different in Scotland from Italy.

Back home one or two players who are friendly with each other will maybe occasionally go to each other's houses for a meal.

At Ibrox everyone socialises much more. Or at least they did in the Gough-McCoist era. Every few weeks, when we didn't have a big game on the Saturday or something, Richard would organise a day out for the team.

I hadn't been there very long when one of these days was organised at TGI Friday's in Glasgow city centre. This was to be my induction.

When I was first told about it I was a bit wary and said I

didn't think I'd like it very much because I'm not a big drinker.

"Rubbish, you'll have a great time," the boys told me, refusing to take no for an answer. And although I was amazed at the amount of drink these guys could consume, I learned so much about the importance of togetherness at a club. It was July, before the season had started, and the boys were ready for a good day out because they'd worked hard in the pre-season training.

All the Italian guys - Rino, Sergio, Marco and I - were there along with a lot of the Scottish boys. Funnily enough, Richard wasn't there that night. But Coisty, Durranty, Andy Goram, Stuart McCall, Charlie Miller and Derek McInnes were and they made sure the captain's beer didn't go to waste.

We were to meet at 5 o'clock and after half an hour I seemed to have more bottles of beer in my hands than I had fingers. That might be an exaggeration but not much of one.

"Guys, I can't drink all these," I remember saying. "I can only drink one or two of these because I need to eat something."

They looked at me as if I had just said the stupidest thing they'd ever heard.

One of them, I can't remember who, said: "Lorenzo, if you eat you won't have enough space in your stomach for drink."

I thought it was a joke. Well, I was the new boy after all.

Before long came the first casualties and I remember a few taxis had to be called after not much more than a couple of hours because some of the lads had been drinking too much too quickly.

I suppose that was a sign of the way this team looked out for one another on and off the pitch.

At most nights out, Richard made sure everyone got home safely. He was a leader in every sense of the word.

He enjoyed himself with the best of them but he was always

making sure that the rest of us were OK at the same time.

He didn't have to worry so much about Lorenzo, though, because I was always determined to stay in control.

Now I must be honest here - I'm no drinker and even if I had developed a taste for Baileys since moving to Scotland I knew I couldn't live with these guys when it came to a night on the town. I knew my body could not take it. In fact it still can't.

So as Jasper Durrant, pushed yet another beer into my hand, I knew I had to come up with some kind of plan. Quickly.

In my desperation I decided to cheat on my team mates.

Every time they bought me a beer I would drink half of it and then pour the rest away or shove it over to the other side of the table. That way they thought I was matching them drink for drink.

I knew that if I kept going at this rate I would be dead in the morning.

At least this way, I calculated, I would only be half dead.

We ended up going out to a club - I think it was the Sky Bar in Archaos - and I will never forget the way I was made to feel that night. Suddenly I began to realise just what it meant to be a Rangers player in Glasgow.

It seemed as if everybody loved us, everybody wanted to talk to us and everybody wanted to buy us more beer - which was just what I needed!

It wasn't only the girls - although it's fair to say I was also realising that as a player in this team I would receive a lot of welcome attention from the fairer sex and I'll tell you more about that side of my life later. But on that particular night it seemed to me the whole city wanted to be our friend.

And all the time I was feeling secretly pleased with myself because none of my team mates had realised that I was not playing fair. Yes, I could hardly wait to see the rest of them at training the next day.

So you can imagine my disappointment, not to mention my astonishment when I turned up the next morning to see them acting as if nothing had happened.

They began to run around the place as if they had been tucked up in bed at half past seven with nothing stronger than a cup of Cocoa.

That was a real eye opener for guys like myself, Rino, Marco and Sergio. We honestly could not believe what we were seeing and to this day I still don't understand how these guys did it.

And then there was Gazza. Now this guy was in a league all of his own.

I remember one afternoon when I was in at the stadium doing a bit of work on my own and trying to keep myself in shape.

It was the day of Walter Smith's testimonial against Liverpool but I wasn't playing. Anyway I was in my seat in the dressing room when in came Gazza wearing a bright yellow jacket and an orange shirt. He was kind of hard to miss.

But when he sat down next to me I realised he didn't just look bad - he smelled awful too. There was a really strong stench of wine and when he took off his jacket I saw he had spilled it all over his shirt. I looked at him and said: "What the hell has happened to you?"

It turned out that his old friend Paul Ince was in town and he had phoned Gazza in the morning - telling him to come up to his hotel with the best bottle of wine in Glasgow.

Gazza went one better. In fact, he went two better.

And so three bottles of wine later here he was in the dressing room - reporting for action.

I asked him if he was seriously going to go out there and play in Walter's game. He just laughed and said: "Why not?"

He did play against Liverpool that night but his days at Ibrox were already numbered.

Much as I loved him - and I still do - I must admit he was becoming too wild. For example I was also there the day he had his infamous run in with poor Erik Bo Andersen.

It's a well known story, of course. We were on the ground doing our stretches when Gazza sneaked up behind Erik and pissed all over him. It really was disgusting.

But what was really incredible was Erik's reaction. He just meekly asked Gazza to stop as if it was just a little joke. I remember thinking to myself if Gazza had done that to me he would have to spend the rest of the day on his hands and knees looking for his teeth.

Gazza had gone too far and yet there was an even more remarkable incident to follow and this one really was the end for him at Rangers.

I think it was around March time and the title was slipping away from us. We had gone to Motherwell and lost 2-1 after Coisty - who was making his own personal late push to save 10-in-a-row - had opened the scoring. Anyway, it was a terrible defeat and one that seemed to push Walter over the edge because on the Monday he was angrier than I had ever seen him before, or since for that matter.

He was furious and he wanted the players to know all about it. "You are throwing this title away to that useless lot across the city", was his message.

And then he began to single out some of the players for special attention. One by one they were dealt with until he reached Gazza.

"And as for you," he said, "you've hardly been sober enough to train properly for the last two weeks..."

Walter had really lost it now. I was certain he was about to punch Gazza in the face. It was an incredible scary sight - in fact, it was too scary for Gazza.

As he sat there I noticed that his trousers were turning a darker colour around his groin. I could not believe what I was seeing. He was actually sitting there pissing himself right before our very eyes.

I can't remember what happened next. I think Walter just walked away and the rest of us did not know what to say.

But I think less than a month later Gazza had gone to Middlesbrough. By the time I was fit enough to begin playing again he was gone and that remains one of my great regrets.

I remember at the start of that season I had made my debut in a pre-season friendly against Everton at Goodison and Gazza, who was injured, watched from the stand sitting next to Glenn Hoddle of all people.

I had to come off because my ankle was troubling me. In fact, although I didn't know it at the time, it was the start of my nightmare but after the game Gazza came up to me and said: "Lorenzo, get well as soon as possible because you looked good out there tonight. I'm looking forward to playing with you."

That meant a lot to me. I had only just arrived at Rangers and here was the great Paul Gascoigne giving me such a compliment.

As well as being my team-mate, he was also my occasional interpreter and I will never forget him. And even although he did some unbelievable things and got himself into a lot of trouble, deep down Gazza always was and still remains a good guy. Don't let anyone tell you any differently.

The truth is all he ever wanted was to be loved and maybe his heart was too big. Yes, he did some stupid things but he was also one of the most generous people I have ever met. Maybe too generous.

But if Gazza wanted to be everybody's friend then there was

another guy in that dressing room who it seemed was only truly happy when he was on his own.

I'm talking of course about Marco Negri.

A lot has been said about my relationship with Marco and I think it is time I put the record straight.

Although, to be honest, I'm still not really sure myself what went so wrong between the two of us. Only Marco Negri really knows the truth.

I remember the way he started that season. He was unbelievable.

I was on the sidelines having more and more problems with my ankle until eventually I left for Italy at the end of September.

But I had already watched Negri score around 20 goals in his first 10 games. I had never seen goal-scoring like this before in all my life.

Of course, some people will dismiss what he did that season and say it is easy to score goals in the Scottish league.

But I have my own ideas about that and I know there is a secret to scoring goals - no matter what league you are scoring them in.

You have to be in the right place at the right moment and Marco had that sixth sense. He was outstanding.

I still believe we would have won the league that season and made history if Marco had not injured himself playing squash with Sergio.

It was a strange accident. The ball hit him in the eye and he was out for a month. Even when he came back he told me he couldn't see properly.

And it was over that period that everything seemed to change for him.

Before that moment I had got on very well with him. We were close.

But I came back from rehabilitation in Italy to discover that all was not well with my friend.

All of a sudden it seemed he didn't feel good about living in Glasgow. He wasn't settled and he was having problems with some of the players.

I can't say what caused these problems because I wasn't around to see for myself. But I heard that he had fallen out with some of the guys, including Sergio and Rino and that he had a little problem with Walter Smith as well.

I think I knew then that there would be trouble. I could see it in training - he wasn't the same player that I had left a few months earlier.

And the situation was to get worse, much worse.

One night we went out - myself, Marco and our girlfriends, Cristina and Monica.

We had gone to the opening of the Rotunda Casino in Glasgow. The owner was an Italian so a big group of us were all invited.

We were having a great night and Marco and I were talking about arranging a trip up to Perth to go clay pigeon shooting.

The plan was for all four of us to go up there together. The girls could keep each other company and go to see some castles while Marco and I were shooting. We were all looking forward to it.

But Monica said she couldn't make it because some of her relatives were supposed to be coming to Glasgow. She said that Marco should go on his own.

When Cristina heard this she said there wasn't much point in her going just to sit around a hotel on her own. She suggested that Marco and I went on our own.

I turned to Marco and said: "That's good for us. We can stay up there on our own and do anything we want!"

The next thing I knew Monica had exploded. I don't know what she thought I meant - maybe she thought I was trying to take Marco away from her or set him up with a new girlfriend.

Whatever it was, she lost the plot. She was screaming and shouting and accusing me of all kinds of things. There were a lot of people around and she was making a real scene. I don't want to say what she called me - hey, there could be kids reading this - but let's just say it was pretty offensive.

I was really embarrassed but I stayed calm because I wanted to respect the owner of the restaurant. The last thing I was going to do was get involved in a shouting match with this crazy girl.

At one point Rino's father turned to me and said: "I don't know how you do it? I would have snapped by now."

But what was the point? This was just a stupid row and I didn't want to get involved. Also, I didn't want to cause any more problems for Marco but little did I know it was already too late.

I don't know if he was affected by what she was saying that night. I don't know if, when they went home she told him to stay away from me.

But something had changed between us and a couple of weeks later our friendship was over forever.

The season had finished - in the worst possible way - and I had returned to Italy for the summer. After a couple of days I got a phone call from a reporter telling me about an interview Negri had done back in Scotland.

It turned out he was accusing me of bad mouthing him to the chairman. I could not believe what I was hearing.

Now let's get this straight. By this time I knew that he was going out drinking quite a lot in Edinburgh. He was not happy and this was his way of dealing with it.

But the last thing I was going to do was to go running to the chairman to tell stories about him. What kind of man did he take me for?

I had a close relationship with David Murray and I still do to this day. But I don't even talk to him about my own private life never mind anyone else's.

So I was furious. I just told the reporter: "Listen, I don't think Mr Murray needs me to tell him that Marco Negri likes getting drunk in Edinburgh."

David Murray lives and works in Edinburgh. In fact he probably owns half of the city.

Is it any surprise that a guy like him - who knows so many people there - finds out that Marco has been running around the place getting drunk?

But to this day I don't know why Marco thought I was the guy who dropped him in it. I still wonder what was going through his head.

I had never gone through a situation quite like it before. I didn't know why Monica had been so strange with me that night and I couldn't believe that Marco was turning against me too.

He never did tell me why. Not once did he try to explain.

If I saw them both on the street today I'd say hello. I don't have to hide because I can look in my heart and know that I did nothing wrong.

But we went a long, long time without saying a single word to one another after that summer.

It bothered me but not that much. I had lived for 27 years quite happily without Marco Negri so I wasn't going to curl up and die now.

It was Marco who had the problem. It was always Marco who had the problems. He began to talk also about conspiracies against him in the dressing room. He thought the other players had it in for him - that they didn't want to let him finish the season as the top scorer in Scotland.

Ally McCoist was still at the club and Marco had convinced himself that the rest of us wanted him to lead the attack.

Again, this theory existed only in one man's head - Marco's.

He believed that the rest of us didn't want to pass the ball to him. What he forgot was that this team was trying to make history.

These players he was accusing were the guys who had carried this great club to the verge of something so very special. They were living and breathing to make it 10-in-a-row.

And somehow Marco thought they would give it all up just to piss him off. I have never heard anything so stupid.

He had problems OK, many, many problems. I don't know if it was the city, his girlfriend or his family but he took it out on all the wrong people.

He turned against his team-mates and there was no way back after that.

Sometimes I wonder if he even enjoyed playing football for a living.

OK, it's time to be very honest with you all again. When I signed for Rangers I was doing it for the money. There, I said it again. It was the same for all of the Italian players. We went to Scotland because of the wages that were being offered.

But Marco made one big mistake - he made no attempt to embrace the culture or to adapt to his new life. He couldn't or wouldn't accept that he was no longer living in Italy.

I'm not saying that Italy is better than Scotland. All I'm saying is that the two countries are different and if you have decided to leave Italy behind then you have to be prepared to make an effort to settle in.

The food, the weather, the habits that the people have -

everything is different and it's your responsibility to get used to it.

Sometimes I think Marco thought that it was everyone else who had to change just to suit him.

Myself, Sergio and Rino were completely different. We got more involved in the social side of things and began to love our new lifestyle. But the more we enjoyed it the more Marco resented it.

Maybe that was his biggest problem but then we are talking about a guy who has had problems everywhere he has been. He had problems at Udinese, he had problems at Cosenza, he had problems at Bologna.

Yes, like I say, Marco Negri is no stranger to turmoil. Don't get me wrong, deep down he's a nice guy but he's a strange guy too. He likes to be on his own and that's not ideal when you are part of a team.

If you can't share your feelings - no matter if they are bad or good - with your team-mates then you won't fit in and feel part of it.

So that was the end of Marco. Of course, he stayed at the club for another three years but he was completely out of the first-team picture.

I kept waiting for him to say sorry or even to explain why he had said these terrible things about me. But the apology never came so we never spoke for a long time.

After a few months he was brought back into training by Dick Advocaat. To be fair, Advocaat asked me first if I had any problems with Marco being part of the squad and I told him it was entirely his decision to make.

In a way I'm glad it happened because slowly we started to talk to each other again. It ended up that we even spent Christmas Day together - believe it or not his girlfriend was there too - and we all got on quite well, talking about things in general.

But there was nothing special between us. There never could be after all that had been said. A couple of months later he agreed a deal with Rangers to release him early from his contract and he returned to Italy.

There were all kinds of rumours about him because he was not a well boy at the time. He had a bone infection and his immune system was not fighting against it.

I have since been told that some people thought he might even have a life threatening illness but I don't believe that. If that was true then I'm sure we would have found out all about it by now.

But what I did know was that the leg infection was very serious. I was told there was a chance he might even have to have it amputated.

Apparently his leg had been ripped open during a reserve game at Aberdeen. The skin had been completely ripped off and so it was impossible for the doctors to put stitches in.

That's what caused the infection to get into the leg.

But I think when he was told by the medical people that he might have to lose the leg he went crazy. Well you would, wouldn't you?

That's why he went back to Italy to be treated and thankfully he got sorted out.

Things might not always have been great between us but I never wanted to see him go through something as terrible as that.

I know he doesn't have a club yet but I'm just pleased for him that he's still walking on two legs.

I just hope, if he ever does find a club again, that he will learn from his mistakes. He should think back to that first season at Ibrox and realise that he made no attempt to be part of our group.

125

And what a group it was.

It was round about November that Walter declared he too would be leaving us. That was another one of those life-changing moments even if I didn't know it at the time.

It was the end of an era at Ibrox and all around me were players who knew that their time here was almost over too.

By January the newspapers were starting to come up with the names of the men who were in with a chance of taking Walter's job. One name kept being mentioned more than any other - Dick Advocaat.

# *Chapter Seven*

## ADVOCAAT RULES

BRIAN LAUDRUP was the first guy in the dressing room to find out what life under Advocaat would be like.

Lauders knew someone in Holland who had played under Advocaat and I remember him warning us about what was in store. He told us that in Holland Advocaat had a reputation for being a very hard man and also a very strange man. I had no idea how right his informant was.

All I knew was that a completely different culture was coming to Rangers Football Club.

I actually met the new boss before any of the others - it was the start of a relationship full of incredible highs and devastating lows.

David Murray had announced officially around March that Advocaat would be taking over from June 1.

I was back at Ibrox early that morning because I had missed seven months of the previous season and I couldn't wait to get started again.

I remember I bumped into him in the corridor. We exchanged the usual polite greetings and he said something about me being taller than he had thought. Nothing too strange there I thought.

About half an hour later I realised that, just this once, my first impression was off the mark. Way off.

By this time we were all gathered in the dressing room and Advocaat was standing there in front of us explaining what he expected from his players.

First he went through the usual stuff - the pre-season programme and these kind of things - but we knew already he was an odd little man. It was the way he spoke. He was poker straight.

It was something of a shock for all of us who had been in that dressing room under Walter Smith. These had been good times - fun times - but already the atmosphere had been transformed. It was clear there wouldn't be many laughs around the place from now on.

And then he started with the rules. Oh my God those rules!

Here we were, a group of grown men - experienced players from all over Europe. There were guys like Ian Ferguson and Gordon Durie who were in their thirties and who had spent the best part of a decade at Ibrox.

And all of a sudden the were sitting there quietly like naughty schoolboys listening to the new headmaster. I remember looking around at the faces as the rules were being listed and thinking to myself that this was unbelievable.

"Guys - I don't like mobile phones. From now on if I see a mobile phone in this dressing room you will be fined £50.

"Anyone using a mobile phone on the team bus will be fined.

"Anyone who turns up here late in the morning will be fined. Anyone who gets on the bus for training late in the morning will be fined. Anyone who is not out on that training field at exactly the right time will be fined."

And then there was my favourite. "The team will eat together and no-body is allowed to start before I say 'enjoy your meal'."

Imagine saying something like that to Ian Ferguson - a 32 year-old man and a legend at this club.

It was like school dinners.

When Advocaat was finished we just looked at each other in total disbelief. I started to laugh - it was all so ridiculous - and then everyone else started too.

Well, it couldn't get any worse we thought. How wrong we were - the rules were only just beginning.

I remember a couple of weeks later we went to Norway on pre-season tour and I was walking through the hotel at lunch-time making my way to the dining room so we could all sit down and wait for the headmaster to give us permission to eat.

I had my T-shirt hanging outside of my shorts. I was about to find out what a bad boy I was.

Advocaat came marching over to me, stopped me and said: "What are you doing? Do you think you are here on holiday?"

I honestly had no idea what he was talking about. So I asked him.

"Put your shirt inside your shorts," he barked back at me with his little eyes bulging, "That's the way to behave yourself.".

I just looked down at him, shook my head and said: "What are you talking about?" I walked away and sat down at my table. I didn't like the way he was talking to me and there was no way I was going to tuck in my T-shirt just because he had told me to.

At the end of lunch he came up to me again. "I need to talk to you," he said. When everybody was away we sat down together.

He told me that he needed players like me in his team. I was an experienced player and I had to set an example to the rest.

I didn't see this one coming. He was sitting there opening his heart to me and telling me about the problems he was facing and how difficult it was going to be for him to build a new team.

He asked me for my help. I said to him I would be happy to help him but I asked him why he wanted to treat us like kids. I asked him what difference he thought it would make to the future success of Rangers Football Club if I tucked my T-shirt into my shorts.

He just said: "I know, but it looks better that way."

So, of course, I tucked it in. I didn't cost me much. Anyway, I was sure these hard rules wouldn't last long. This was just his way of bringing us together and getting us to move in the same direction. It would all be over soon, I thought to myself.

But he never changed. In fact, he got worse and worse.

Even when we were winning trophy after trophy in those first two seasons he would come up with more and more rules.

At first we were allowed to use our mobile phones immediately after games. After one year he told us that had to stop too.

There were so many rules it was hard to keep up. I can't even remember half of them now.

There was one, though, which always got right up my nose.

I have always trained wearing Bermuda shorts - or cycling shorts as you would call them - because I have big thighs and these shorts help to keep my muscles warm.

But he wouldn't allow it. If I wanted to wear Bermudas then I had to wear a pair of normal shorts on top of them or even a tracksuit. I found that uncomfortable but that didn't matter to Advocaat. All that mattered were his rules.

As a group of players we were under pressure. At a club like Rangers you are always in the spotlight. That's the life of an Old Firm player.

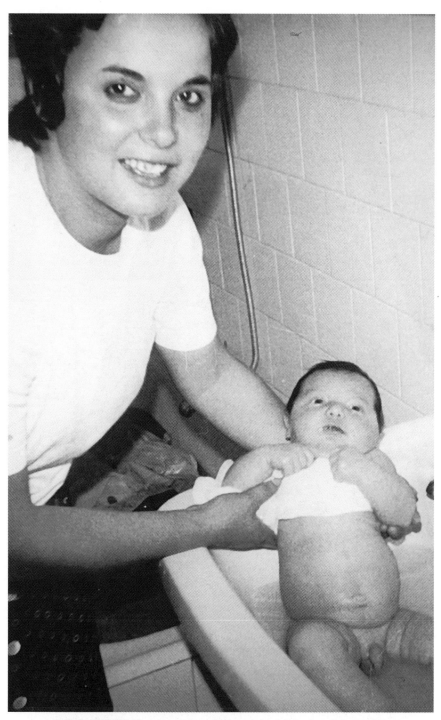

**BATH TIME:** Lorenzo aged 6 months showing his tackle.
He claims things have developed significantly since then.

**MASK OF LORENZO:** eat your heart out Catherine Zeta.

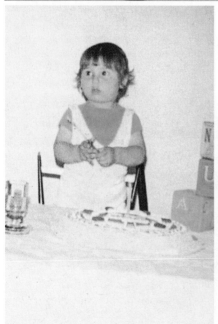

**YOUTH SYSTEM:** cycling with my brother Davide (top) on my 1st Birthday (left) and playing with my first football aged only 10 months! (right)

**FAMILY MAN:** me with mum, dad and the rest of the family.

**ITALIAN STALLION:** my new Ferrari with Florence in the background.

**STARTING OUT:** a fresh-faced young striker with hometown team Bari.

**MOVING ON:** playing with Fiorentina in Serie A was a dream come true.

**HOMETOWN BOY:** back home in Bari with my dad Mauro.

**WASH DAY BLUES:** mum and dad hanging out my collection of shirts.

**AMO'S BEST FRIEND:** a hug for my lovely dog Pako.

**SHOOTING STAR:** on the moors with my friend Vito Laviola.

**TAKING AIM:** shooting and fishing helps me to relax.

**WELCOME TO IBROX:** with Rangers chairman David Murray, top, and Staale Stensaas, bottom, who signed on the same day.

**TREBLE TRIUMPH:** me with the silverware Rangers won in 1999 – the SPL Championship Trophy, the League Cup and the Scottish Cup, top, and with my Ibrox teammates as we celebrate our achievement.

**CHAMPION FEELING:** holding aloft the SPL Trophy in 2000.

**SPRAY IT AGAIN:** a champagne moment with Barry Ferguson, Billy Dodds, Neil McCann and Jorg Albertz after our 2000 league triumph.

**RACE RIOT:** a tussle with Borussia Dortmund players. Afterwards I was accused of being racist… but that's certainly not the case.

**NOT SEEING EYE TO EYE:** Dick Advocaat stripped me of the captaincy.

**HOLD ME BACK:** Dick shouts the odds as I'm sent off against Hearts.

**OLD PALS ACT:** but Arthur Numan and I had words.

**AMERICAN DREAM:** relaxing in Florida during a pre-season tour.

**TRAINING DAY:** I enjoy my time working hard before a big game.

**MODEL PROFESSIONAL:** well at least the clothes look good!

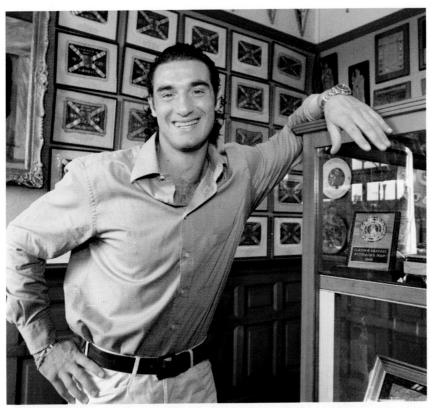

**HAPPY DAYS:** here I am in the famous Ibrox trophy room.

**PLAYER OF THE MONTH:** I picked up my award back in February 2002.

**PASTA MY BEST:** in the kitchen preparing a delicious Italian dish.

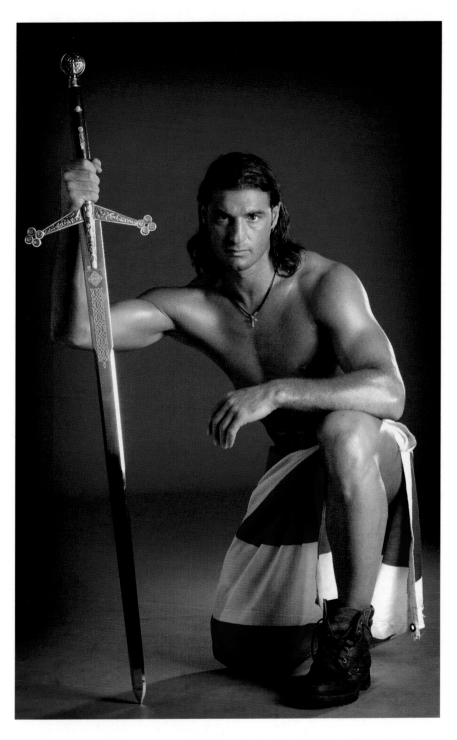

**BRAVEHEART:** wrapped in the colours of my adopted homeland.

**TEAM TALK:** Alex McLeish gave us back our spirit and a will to win.

**VICTORY PARADE:** me with the CIS Cup after we beat Ayr last season.

**CUP OF CHEER:** celebrating the 2002 Scottish Cup win with manager Alex McLeish, above, and the festivities continue, below.

So the last thing we needed was to be treated like children. We would go out there and win matches for him and when we came off he would be standing there with the whip in one hand and the rulebook in the other.

He wouldn't even give us freedom to think. It was his way or no way and so, even although we had started the season really well, the atmosphere in the dressing room was not the best.

Under Walter if we didn't like something then we were free to say so. We would have meetings and if we felt that something wasn't right it was our chance to take it up with the manager. I'm happy to say it's the same now at Murray Park under Alex McLeish but Advocaat simply never let up. Even when we were going well he could not bring himself to loosen the noose which was strangling the spirit of the team.

I'll give you another example...although this time, to his disgust, he had to give in.

It came in his third season. We had won the championship the previous two years but for some reason Advocaat felt that the shorts we had been wearing were too long.

In his opinion the baggy look did not make us appear athletic enough. I don't know - we were athletic enough to win five trophies out of six wearing them.

Anyway, he contacted Nike and ordered them to send us tighter fitting, 'shorter' shorts. Now that was okay for some of the guys but for others like Jorg and me who have big thighs it was just ridiculous.

The shorts clung to us and restricted our movement. They were also far too short. When Tore Andre Flo joined us I felt sorry for him because his legs were so long that the shorts looked preposterous on him.

Eventually, enough was enough. I went to see the manager and told him: "Look, we can't play in these shorts. They are no good to us."

Initially Advocaat refused to do anything about it but we kept chipping away at him and at Jimmy Bell the kit man. Jimmy takes a real pride in his work and is very good at providing us with everything we need but when we were moaning at him about the shorts he took it personally. He thought we were criticising him, which wasn't the case because we all know he does his best for us.

I don't know if Jimmy spoke to Advocaat about it but eventually a consignment of longer, more comfortable shorts arrived at Ibrox. Advocaat didn't say anything about it but he let us wear them. It should never have been an issue, though, but with Advocaat there is no talking. Not unless you are telling him how much you agree with his decisions.

In a recent interview Advocaat said Lorenzo was a player who had too much to say for himself. He made me out to be a hot-head because I spoke up for myself and for my team mates.

He makes out that he has an open mind and that he can accept other people's point of view. Yes, that's right - but only if those opinions are exactly the same as his own. If not he will not even take them into consideration.

So I suppose there was never any chance that he and I would have a good relationship. Right from the start there was too much friction between us.

It also didn't matter to him that his rules were costing people money - and not just in fines. I'm talking about serious money here.

Advocaat had bought Gabriel Amato that first summer. It was a great piece of business because Amato was a top player in Spain. He was so good Adidas paid him fortunes to wear white boots.

But not at Ibrox. Not as long as Dick Advocaat and his rule book were around.

"You're not wearing them here," he snapped at Gabriel, "If you wear those boots you won't be playing in my team."

Now Gabby didn't speak great English and I did a lot of translating for him.

I think he knew what Advocaat was saying to him but he looked at me in utter astonishment. I think he was hoping it was a simple mis-understanding. He wasn't really hearing this.

But he was. "I like black and white boots," Advocaat continued, "You can have a label on them but that's all. No-one will wear coloured boots here."

I could almost see out of the corner of my eye Rino Gattuso sliding his blue boots under the dressing room bench. Jorg Albertz was also supposed to wear white boots that season but not any more.

To be honest this was something I couldn't accept. This was another one of those rules that I felt I had to take a stance against.

What difference did it make what colour Gabby's boots were if he was scoring the goals that were winning us games?

This was one of those fights I couldn't walk away from. I stood up and said: "Listen, Gabby is wearing those boots because he's being paid a lot of money. If you don't like them then you tell the chairman to make up the difference in his wages.

"If you can't do that then you go and find him another sponsor who will pay him exactly the same money to wear black boots."

I was burning up inside with anger and injustice. I just found this so unfair and so petty that I had to have my say.

Advocaat didn't want to know. He did what he always did when I challenged one of his rules.

He reminded me that he was the manager and that we were all being well paid to play for him. "If I say it - you do it."

That's what he did when he knew he was wrong. He couldn't give a reasoned argument and this was his last resort.

It was his way of saying if you take this any further you will pay for it with your Rangers career. I didn't like him but I wasn't going to walk away from Rangers over it. He wasn't that important.

Maybe he didn't understand just how much this club was beginning to mean to me.

I know I have a hard character. Sometimes I can even be nasty and if I don't like something then I will answer back.

But at the end of every day when I go to bed at night at least I know deep inside that my conscience is clear.

If I have to tell you to something forcibly then that's what I'll do. I'll tell you straight to your face.

What I won't do is get somebody else to do my dirty work for me or to hide behind excuses. If I have a problem with you then I'll be right in your face.

If everyone in football was like that then this would be a better world. Unfortunately there are too many people in this game who shake you with one hand and stab you in the back with the other.

These people don't like the truth. They don't like it if someone criticises them. All they want is for people to tell them how wonderful they are. This is not just Dick Advocaat I'm talking about - the game is full of them.

So when they hear someone who speaks the truth they tend to get scared. I can't stand these people.

Throughout my life I have always tried to be an honest person, first and foremost with myself. If I make a mistake then I am the first one to put my hand in the air and say sorry, that was my fault. There is no shame in admitting when you are wrong. We are all human beings and from time to time we all make mistakes.

We are not invincible and we are not robots.

But Dick Advocaat didn't see things that way. Sure he has a lot of experience as a manager but his biggest weakness is this burning inner belief that he knows everything. When you think like that you show disrespect to almost everyone you come across in the game - you might not mean to but you do. You can't help it.

For example, recently Advocaat said that when he arrived at Ibrox there were only three players left at the club - myself, Sergio and Jorg.

That is a terrible thing for a coach to say. What kind of message does that send out about the other players who were at the club when he came? Players like Barry Ferguson, Ian Ferguson, Rino Gattuso, Jonatan Johansson. The list goes on and on.

But then that's Advocaat all over. The man has an excuse for every situation. He will blame anything and anyone for his own mistakes. Just don't ask him to admit that he got it wrong.

You know, in all my time in Scotland I can't remember ever hearing or reading Advocaat say that he made a mistake. Four years without making one single mistake? The man must be some kind of genius.

No, I don't think that's the way a really good manager behaves. Truly great leaders are those who criticise themselves and learn from where they have gone wrong. How can you learn from your own mistakes when you operate in the belief you have never, ever made one?

I'm sure he still thinks he was right to treat us like kids. I'm sure he's not the slightest bit embarrassed when he thinks back to asking his assistant, Bert van Lingen to sit on the bus every morning with a stop watch to make sure no-one was even one second late.

No, I'm not joking. Everything we did was timed. If you were getting on the bus and then realised you had left something in the dressing room - trainers, tape, shin guards, whatever - you would have to sprint back to get what you needed. One second late and you were fined.

It was ridiculous. I have never gone through such humiliation in all my career as I did with Advocaat.

No-body was happy about it but we put up with it because we realised these were the conditions of the new manager. To be honest I could even see what he was trying to do when it came to being punctual because he wanted his players to show some respect.

But this was way over the top. Stopwatches, boots, shorts, T-shirts and a guide on how and when to eat dinner? It was pathetic.

And yet for a while it worked although I believe that was in spite of these rules rather than because of them.

He had brought in Arthur Numan and Giovanni van Bronckhorst - two excellent signings - and we were flying as a team.

I guess it was the start of Advocaat's attempt to turn Ibrox into a Dutch colony but it was working well. Everyone spoke English in the dressing room and there was a good atmosphere between all of the players.

Of course, there would be the odd argument but no more or no less than you would get at any other club.

I had a little fight with Jorg during a game at Kilmarnock because I took a free kick and didn't make a good job of it. He got angry and we snapped at each other but it was over in seconds. We were winning and a winning team is a happy team.

We had one real blip when we lost 5-1 to Celtic (at the risk of sounding like the former manager I'd like to point out that I was suspended for that game) but we were already ahead of them in the league and we would get stronger and stronger as the season went on.

We were playing a completely new style of football and we should give credit to Advocaat for that. He totally transformed the way Rangers played the game and introduced a more European style with a lot of quick passing.

We didn't have an Ally McCoist to lead our attack either so it was up to everyone to weigh in with some goals and it made us a very exciting team to watch. It was good fun on and off the park.

We were on our way to a Treble and all the time I was becoming very attached to that armband.

To be honest I was stunned the day that Advocaat told me he wanted me to captain this new team. We were at a hotel in Liverpool at the time preparing for a UEFA Cup tie against Shelbourne which had been moved from Dublin to Tranmere's stadium.

We had actually just got back from that pre-season camp in Norway during which we had played a lot of friendlies. In every game the captain was a different player - myself, Jorg, Sergio, Durie and Ian Ferguson - he gave everyone a chance.

But I had no idea that he saw Lorenzo as captain material until the night before we faced Shelbourne.

I was in my room when the phone went. It was Advocaat. He said he needed to talk to me right away in his room.

I have to tell the truth, I went there thinking: "What now?" Had I been wearing the wrong socks at breakfast or did he have a problem with my aftershave?

So you can imagine my surprise when he said: "Listen, for two months now I have been watching you. You have worked hard for the team and the club and you have a very strong character. For those reasons I'm going to make you my captain. What do think about that?"

I was speechless. Not only had I been arguing with him all summer but I had done almost nothing for the team in my first season at the club. I had maybe only played five or six games as a Rangers player.

Jorg had been there for three years, Ian Ferguson was a legend and a Scot and Arthur Numan had been Advocaat's skipper when they were together at PSV Eindhoven. And yet he wanted me.

After I had taken it all in I said: "Thank you very much boss. I really appreciate this."

He said we had to work together to make this team great and I said I would do anything. Any co-operation he needed he would get. And I was deadly serious. This man had just given me the greatest honour of my life. "Let's do it!" I said. I was on such a huge high.

That night at dinner he told everyone that I was the captain and that Arthur would be the vice captain. And so our adventure began.

The next day we faced Shelbourne. To this day I still think it was the most incredible game I have ever played in my life.

It was supposed to be an easy introduction to the UEFA Cup for our new side but, in fact, it nearly killed us before we had even been born.

I still don't know what went wrong but for some reason we found ourselves 2-0 down at half time. We had missed a few chances of our own but it was so obvious that we were the better team. We were so much stronger than our opponents it was unbelievable.

At half time I remember trying to make sense of it all - we all were - and then I think, when we couldn't come up with an answer, we began to get scared. It was as if the Gods were against this new team of ours.

I tried to lift the morale by telling everyone if we could just score one away goal then we could get out of here, back to Glasgow and then finish the job off at Ibrox.

So we went back out full of good intentions - and then lost another goal after something like 10 minutes.

"Oh my God. This can't be happening! Not today! Not to me!"

You have to remember this was my first game as the captain of Glasgow Rangers. Me, Lorenzo Amoruso, an Italian and a Roman Catholic.

No-body had actually come out and said that they didn't like the idea of a Catholic captaining Rangers but I was not stupid. I could read between the lines.

And here we were being destroyed by a bunch of part-time players from Dublin. This was turning into the biggest disaster of my career. I remember deciding right there and then that this armband was not for me. Absolutely not.

But then the manager put on Amato and suddenly our luck changed. I think Gabby scored our first goal and from that moment on there was no way Shelbourne could stop us. We ended up winning that game 5-3 and it was maybe the biggest relief I had ever known in football.

We had escaped and we were to go from strength to strength but it wasn't all roses and chocolates.

We were a little bit shaky in the beginning and I knew my own form was not so good either because I had found it hard coming back after so long on the sidelines the previous season.

Yes, I had problems and the fans were not so slow to notice. Some of them - no, most of them - didn't seem to like me very much at all. Maybe some of them were unhappy that I had been made captain and especially now that the season had started and I was struggling to find my sharpness.

I could sense that they were not convinced but the more I tried to win them over the worse my situation seemed to become. And then came Parma.

Having survived Shelbourne we were paired with Alberto Malesani's side in the UEFA Cup. I was really excited about this opportunity to show everyone back in Italy that I had made the right decision in coming to Glasgow.

But, after drawing the first leg 0-0 in Glasgow, it was all to go disastrously wrong. Myself and Sergio were even accused of deliberately sabotaging our European campaign as some kind of favour for our countrymen.

We were 1-0 up when Sergio was sent off and then I gave away a ridiculous penalty with a handball inside our own penalty box. Even now I don't know why I did it - I was ahead of Enrico Chiessa as we chased a ball towards the by-line. There was no great danger but for some reason my instincts told me to stick out a hand.

So I suppose I knew that I would be slaughtered for this and so did Sergio. They said it was an Italian job but these stupid people didn't ever pause to consider just how much it would have meant to Sergio and myself to get one over on an Italian club. We would have given our blood to make that happen.

Thankfully, Advocaat did not hold it against me. He just asked me why I did it and I shook my head and told him the truth: "I have no idea."

He accepted that because he is a football man and that was one of those incidents that maybe only people who have played the game will ever understand. But the fans were a different story altogether. We lost that game 3-1 and there was no argument over who was to blame.

It was sickening and made all the harder to take as we knew that, if Sergio had stayed on the park, then we might pulled off a wonderful result. At that time Parma had a very strong team - strong enough to be fighting for the league title in Italy. I think they went on to win the UEFA Cup that season, beating Marseille 3-0 in the final so that shows the quality we were up against.

Then again, that's probably why the supporters were so upset. They knew how close we had come to something very special and, when it fell apart they lashed out at the men they held responsible. I was an obvious target.

Soon after that Colin Hendry was signed from Blackburn and a lot of people thought he would be taking over as the leader of our team. After all, he was the captain of Scotland.

The truth is I still don't know what really happened with Colin. It's been said that he was the chairman's choice and even that David Murray promised him that, if he agreed to come to

Ibrox, he would be given my armband.

All I do know is that this appeared to be a huge gift from the chairman direct to the supporters. He had delivered the captain of Scotland.

But in my heart of hearts I was never too worried because the manager told me right from the start that he would not change his decision.

That was good to know but it was still a very bad time for me. I knew I wasn't playing well and I knew a lot of the supporters were pushing for Colin instead of me.

But I didn't have time to feel sorry for myself. I had to win them over as quickly as possible and as the season went on the better our relationship became.

I worked hard to show them that this was not the real Lorenzo Amoruso. I knew what I could give to this club and I knew I had been letting myself down. My head was sound but my legs were weak so I decided to work harder than ever before to get myself into shape.

It had been a rough October for me but by the end of November we had won the CIS Cup - beating St Johnstone at Celtic Park to win my first trophy as captain - and from then on things would get better and better.

We had a good winter break in America and when we returned we were on fire, playing some unbelievable football. We won something like eight or nine games in a row and opened up a big gap at the top of the table.

But we weren't over the finishing line yet and, after we picked up a lot of injuries, Celtic began to eat into our lead until it was down to just seven points.

And then it was time to go to Parkhead for 90 minutes which would send shock waves through the entire footballing world.

I'll be honest here. We were a bit worried about this one. There were only four games to go and we knew if we lost then Celtic would be right back in it. The pressure had been piled on us all week and on top of that we knew we had not been playing well.

I remember sitting in that dressing room before kick-off. Hardly anyone said a word. I looked around and saw the looks on the faces of my team-mates. We were all nervous because we had a lot of responsibility on our shoulders and it was a very heavy atmosphere.

But when the whistle sounded it was as if we were released. Suddenly we were back at the top of our game and after something like five minutes Neil McCann had put us in front when he stretched to get his left foot on the end of a great cross from Rod Wallace.

We didn't look back. We knew this was our day and that there was nothing this Celtic side could do to stop us. Unfortunately so did the Celtic supporters.

After about 20 minutes we won a corner which Jorg took. At the back post Mark Viduka and Tony Vidmar were standing almost on their own. I remember it all so clearly.

The ball seemed to take forever to drop out of the air but as it came down Viduka pulled on Tony's shirt and Hugh Dallas had no choice but to give us a penalty. Everybody had seen it because the pair of them were isolated and the ball had been dropping straight onto Tony's head.

The referee had to give a penalty and he did. And then all hell broke lose.

The fans had seen enough and they decided to take matters into their own hands. Down came the coins from such a height that they were more like bullets. Even when Dallas had been struck by one and when the blood began to pour from his head, they did not stop.

Myself and some of the other players tried to protect Dallas as he fell onto one knee. He was dazed and the coins just kept on coming. What else could we do?

We tried to take him away from that area and let the medical people deal with the situation. It was a terrible, terrible moment for football.

These pictures were being beamed out all over the world and the whole of Scotland was being shamed. It was totally embarrassing.

I remember thinking that the game was certain to be abandoned but - even although some fans then tried to get onto the pitch to attack him - Dallas handled it very, very well and refused to do the easy thing.

It would have been so easy for him to walk away and leave the authorities to clean up this mess but he was incredibly brave.

I mean, there were people falling out of the top tier of the stadium for God's sake. It was like a bad dream. I saw that guy fall onto the people below as did a lot of the players because there was a break in play at the time.

It was horrible and the atmosphere was getting nastier and nastier all of the time. The feeling was that Celtic's supporters were trying to get the game stopped because they found it entirely unacceptable for Rangers to win back their title at their own stadium.

But, after Jorg had finally scored that penalty we knew we had the opportunity to crush their spirits completely. Perhaps if we had allowed Celtic to come back at us then their supporters might have got even more excited and even more volatile.

But right at the start of the second half Neil scored his second goal to put us 3-0 up and they knew then it was all over.

I still think about that day and about what Dallas did. He probably knew that if he chose to walk off he could have started a riot. Not only that but I believe he acted for the good of the game in this country. I believe he didn't want to have to abandon a game under these circumstances because he knew it would do even more damage to the reputation of Scottish football.

He had every right to stop it because, trust me, he was losing a lot of blood. But he kept it going and he made the right decision.

By the time it was all over most of the Celtic fans had left the ground which was a good thing because, as we celebrated the victory which had won us the league, I decided we should form a huddle on the touchline.

Of course, you won't believe this but I never meant it as in insult. Honestly, the thought didn't even cross my mind that this was a Celtic trademark as it was something we used to do in the dressing room at Fiorentina - a sign of our unity in adversity.

But the Celtic fans didn't take it well. They ran towards the tunnel as we were going off and some of the things they shouted at me would make your hair curl.

But that didn't bother me one bit. Why should it? These people had been threatening me and speaking to me like this ever since I first arrived in Scotland. I knew they hated me and that deep down they saw me as some kind of traitor. The truth is I was delighted to see them hurting so badly.

You see, every time they sing stupid songs about me it makes me stronger and more determined to put them down. Until the day I leave Rangers I will try to give them a difficult time.

And on that particular day it could not have been any worse for them. When we got into the dressing room we went wild. The champagne was everywhere as well as the beer and wine and we were jumping around in it all, kissing and cuddling each other. It was a great celebration - one of the best feelings I've had in my life.

I understood exactly what it meant for Rangers to win that title at Celtic's home ground. I knew we were making history. We had destroyed them completely and I knew this was something big, something very big.

All that was left was for us to finish the job by beating Celtic again in the Scottish Cup Final at Hampden. It seemed that no-one really thought we would do it as so many big names in the papers and on the television were saying we wouldn't be hungry enough.

But I remember that game as if it was yesterday. It was outstanding.

Near the end I blocked a shot from Paul Lambert with my chest. We were 1-0 up through a Rod Wallace goal but Celtic were demanding a penalty kick because they thought I had stopped the shot with my arm.

My heart was in my mouth as I looked over towards the referee. It was Hugh Dallas.

Now was his big chance to level things up and maybe to win over the people he had upset at Celtic Park a couple of weeks earlier. I'm sure a weaker man would have caved in.

But Dallas is not a weak man. He knew it had hit me on the chest and he turned down Celtic's claims. The TV pictures proved later that he had got it right and after the game I thanked him for being so strong and so honest.

Then the party started. I was so happy I even told Tony Vidmar that we would both grab Advocaat after the presentation and throw him up in the air. Everyone joined in and it was a magical moment.

In fact, it was a day I will cherish forever. I still have my man of the match award in my living room and my armband is wrapped around it. On the inside of the armband is written one word: TREBLE.

I had come through a lot that season but I had ended it with the highest moment of my career.

I suppose I should have known I couldn't stay up there forever.

# *Chapter Eight*

## AMO A RACIST? NEVER

WE were the kings of Scotland and it was now time for us to conquer Europe. At least, that was the plan.

We were setting off on another incredible adventure which would take us from Finland back to Parma of all places and then on to the holy grail of the Champions League. But for me our travels were to end in disgrace when I was caught on camera calling an opponent a "black b*****d". And this time I had no-one but myself to blame.

Yet everything had started so well when I scored in the first game of the season away to FC Haka. New boy Michael Mols also scored in that game and the team looked fantastic with him leading our attack.

Michael had arrived in the summer from Utrecht for £4million. Another Dutchman but a quality striker who made an instant impact.

We had travelled to Finland knowing that Parma were waiting for us in the next qualification round which was not a nice thought after what had happened to us over there the previous year.

Here we go again I thought to myself. Just when we needed a bit of luck we were facing up to another match against players like Juan Sebastian Veron, Ariel Ortega, Hernan Crespo and Lillian Thuram.

But we were ready to take on anybody by then and when Parma came to Glasgow they were blown away.

Our fans were incredible. I had never known noise like that in my life before. We were trying to speak to each other on the park but even from as close as three yards away you couldn't hear a word that was being said.

I could feel the blood pumping around my veins faster than ever before. This was our moment - I just knew it.

Parma's players were not prepared for this. They were scared by the atmosphere and surprised with the high tempo of our play. I looked into the eyes of these players and I could almost see the panic.

After no more than 20 minutes Fabio Cannavaro had been sent off. He simply could not live with Rod Wallace and that summed up their entire team. We were beating them all over the pitch and there was nothing they could do to stop us.

Tony Vidmar scored a great goal to put us in front but we really should have been three or four goals up by half-time. It was the same after the break but eventually we had to settle for a

2-0 win with Claudio Reyna scoring the only goal of the second half.

I was happy but not ecstatic. We had missed an opportunity to kill Parma off in 90 minutes and now we had to go back to Italy - to the very place I had left a year ago with my reputation badly damaged.

Sergio Porrini felt the same way. Together we had been accused of selling our souls to let Parma stay in the UEFA Cup and now, 12 months later, the pressure was on us again.

My dad even felt the pressure because he had been at that first game and he knew how badly I had taken that defeat.

So in the build up to this one he wanted to keep me informed about everything that was being said back home in Italy.

One day he called me and told me to switch on my fax machine. He had something I needed to see.

It was an article in which the Parma manager Alberto Malesani was pin-pointing the Rangers defence as the weakest area of our team. He had the cheek to say that Parma would qualify easily because they would score at least three or four goals against us.

Hernan Crespo, who had missed the first game, was coming back for the return leg and Malesani was convinced he would murder us.

I could not have wished for a bigger incentive. I could not believe the lack of respect he was showing us and I took that fax into training the next day to show the rest of the guys. We were all furious and determined to ram those words back down Malesani's throat.

What we didn't realise was that our own manager also had a surprise in store. All of a sudden when he arrived in Italy he announced that he was adopting a new system - he wanted us to go man for man.

I had to take care of Crespo, Sergio was told to look after

Marco Di Viao and it was down to Barry Ferguson to keep Ortega quiet. Craig Moore was given a free role as sweeper.

What a time to make such a change. We had never played like this before. Was this guy for real?

The good thing was that at least myself and Sergio had plenty experience of playing this way from our time in Italy.

But I have to admit – it worked like a dream. We completely controlled Crespo, Ortega and Di Viao. It was like we had knocked out Parma's teeth and we got to half time at 0-0.

After the break Tony Vidmar hit the bar with an amazing shot and we were in great shape until, with five minutes to go, Lionel Charbonnier let a really bad free kick go through him and into the net.

I remember thinking to myself: "Come on Lorenzo, just five more minutes. That's all we need. Don't let it go wrong again."

When I heard the treble blast of the referee's whistle I sank to the ground. We had done it. I looked around and the scenes were incredible. The Rangers fans were going crazy and the players were jumping and screaming.

An Italian TV crew came up to me, shoved a camera in my face and started asking about what had gone wrong with Parma. The interview was going out live on Italian TV.

I said: "If you want to talk to me then let's talk about Rangers."

I wasn't going to stand there and break my heart about knocking an Italian team out of Europe. I told them: "Believe me, the satisfaction I feel right now is double just because it is Parma we have knocked out."

I didn't mention what Malesani had been saying before the game but I wanted to. I just said there were one or two things that had been said in the newspapers that I didn't like.

I knew Malesani would get the message.

Anyway, I just wanted to join in the celebrations. We had made it into the Champions League and at the same time we had gained revenge for what had happened here one year earlier. It was a wonderful victory.

Now we were faced with Valencia, Bayern Munich and PSV Eindhoven. We were ready for anything.

The first game was against Valencia who were struggling in La Liga and everybody was talking up our chances when we arrived in Spain. But we got off to a terrible start in the Mestalla. It was 0-0 at half-time but we were lucky to be in the game. We were struggling with the heat and playing very baldy and so when we lost a goal at the start of the second half we were finished.

They scored again to win the match 2-0 but we felt we could bounce back and we were right.

The next game, against Bayern, came only a week later but it has stuck in my throat ever since.

Everything was going perfectly. We were well organised and had taken the lead through a Jorg Albertz goal. Then Michael Mols had another two or three chances. We could easily have been four or fives goals up but once again we made life hard for ourselves and we had to pay a heavy price.

Bayern cheated the referee to win a free-kick on the edge of our box. There were only three or four minutes to go but we should have known what was coming next. Michael Tarnat took it - it smashed off one of his own players and flew into our net. It was devastating.

I still look back at that game as the one that ultimately cost us qualification for the second phase of the Champions League although for a while it looked as if we might get there anyway.

We went to Eindhoven next and the big news before the game was that Advocaat had dropped Jorg Albertz. None of us knew why but I did know that Jorg took it very badly. He had been playing so well and scoring a lot of goals and now, when it mattered more than ever, he was left watching from the bench. I felt so sorry for him.

But we couldn't argue with Advocaat and so we went out into battle without our biggest weapon. We actually played a good game but we just couldn't find a way through.

Myself and Craig Moore were handling Ruud van Nistelrooy and Luc Nilis very, very well but it just didn't look as if we were going to get the goal we needed to win it. And then on came Jorg.

It seemed as if he had only just came on when we broke away on a counter attack through Michael Mols. The ball broke to Jorg on the left hand side of the box and BANG. We had done it.

Jorg lost control for a second or two. He ran towards the Rangers fans and pointed to the name on the back of his shirt. All his emotion, all his anger, was coming out. It was a strange reaction but I knew how he felt and I was delighted both for Jorg and for the team. This was the break we needed.

PSV came to Ibrox next and we destroyed them 4-1. I scored from a corner with a header and we ended the night at the top of the group. It really was a great night and I began to feel that anything might be possible for this team.

But Advocaat was about to make a big mistake just when qualification was in our grasp. When Valencia came to Ibrox he used the same system as he had against PSV - with Derek McInnes keeping his place as a defensive midfield player.

Derek had come in from no-where for that match against PSV and had been outstanding but this was another team with a completely different style of play and they tore us apart.

We were 2-0 down at half-time and although Craig Moore pulled one back in the second half we never looked liked getting the result we needed and so it all came down to the final match in the Olympic Stadium in Munich. We went there needing a draw to go through which is never an easy task for any team.

We were tense and it showed. In the first 15 minutes Giovanni van Bronckhurst gave away a penalty and they scored, leaving us in big, big trouble.

But something seemed to click after that because as soon as we lost that goal we started to play as if we did not have a care in the world. Michael was leading us from the front and he was an inspiration to us all.

We hit the cross bar and the post and Oliver Kahn was making one unbelievable save after another. But, sadly, Kahn did not stop there.

Before half-time he had made the tackle which destroyed Michael's career. Even now I can shut my eyes and see it perfectly - Kahn racing out of his goal and sliding into Michael out on the touchline. It was quite an awkward challenge but the thing which makes the memory so bitter is that Michael only damaged his knee because he was trying so desperatley not to stamp on Kahn as he fell to the ground.

If he had put his leg down straight then he would have landed on Kahn but his knee would not have buckled the way it did. But Michael is too nice a guy for that.

This was one of the greatest injusticies I have ever known. Michael, over that period, was unreal. Thinking back to those games against Parma for example I have never seen Thuram in so much trouble as he was just trying to live with Michael Mols. No-one could touch him.

After those games it seemed everyone in Italy wanted to know about Michael. I had phonecalls from old team-mates and journalists - everybody wanted to know who this incredible player was and how we had managed to get him to Glasgow.

But Michael was to get even better and when we arrived in Germany he began to hit new heights. At one stage he even nut-megged Lothar Matthaus in the Bayern penalty box. They simply did not know how to stop him.

Maybe Kahn had his own ideas but I doubt it. It was a heavy challenge but I don't really believe it was his intention to take Michael out of the game. It was just a terrible moment.

Even without Michael we continued to cause them problems but the vital equaliser just would not come. We were out of the Champions League and we had lost our new striker. It was a black, black night.

I remember after the game Franz Beckenbauer was interviewed and Stefan Klos stood in our dressing room translating what he was saying. He admitted that Rangers were the far better team and that Bayern Munich didn't deserve to go through.

The funny thing was we were being complimented by one of the greatest names in football but every word he said made me feel sick to my stomach. It was such a sad night but as usual we couldn't feel sorry for ourselves - we didn't have enough time.

We got back to Glasgow with two days to prepare for a vital Old Firm game in the league. Thankfully we reacted strongly to our disappointment, winning 4-2 at Ibrox, and really from that game on things were pretty comfortable for us in the league.

But we were still in Europe in the UEFA Cup and it was on another foreign trip that I was to bring shame on myself and on my club.

After beating Borussia Dortmund at home 2-0 we were going to Germany on a high. Borussia really didn't look too good at Ibrox and, after our performances in the Champions League, we were very confident of completing the job in the second leg.

But we blew it. We were seconds away from going through when we lost a goal with the last kick of the match to take the tie into extra-time and we eventually went out in the sorest possible way - on penalties.

That was bad enough but my problems were only just

beginning. On my way to the airport I received a phonecall from a journalist friend of mine who was back in Glasgow. He told me the TV cameras had clearly showed me calling Victor Ikpeba a "black b*****d" during the game.

I was shocked. Yes, I knew I had been arguing with Ikpeba during the match but I would never have said anything like that, would I? I know this might sound hard to believe but to this day I honestly can't remember saying that.

Sure, I'm no angel and I think nothing of offending other players in the heat of the battle. Some very bad things are said on the football field. But "black b*****d"? That was different. It's just not in my nature to behave like that.

And that's exactly what I told the journalist. This was wrong. Somebody has made a terrible mistake.

But it was me who had made the mistake. When I arrived back in Scotland it was already a big, big story. People were using the video evidence and getting professional lip-readers to study what I had said.

I couldn't believe it but when I looked at the tape myself, suddenly I realised that it looked very bad indeed. To this day I swear that I can't remember saying it but looking at the tape it seemed clear enough even to myself. This was a big, big problem.

I was branded a racist in the papers and I felt everyone turn against me once again. I found that hard to accept because, first of all, I am no racist and the people who really know me know that I don't think like that.

My God, I lived with a black guy from Colombia for three-and-a-half months when I was playing for Bari just to try to help teach him Italian and settle into the area.

For the record I want to state here one more time that I do not have a single racist bone in my body. I deplore racism in all its forms.

So the idea that I hated black people was ridiculous but now this was the big story and I was being hounded. I felt as if they were trying to make me look like someone from the Klu Klux Klan.

Listen, anyone who has played football knows what is said in the heat of the moment. I have lost count of the amount of times I have been called an Italian b*****d on pitches all around Scotland. It still happens now on more or less a weekly basis.

It's something I have learned to accept. It doesn't make me believe that half of the players in the Premierleague want to see all the Italians in Scotland rounded up and sent back across the Meditteranean on the first boat.

OK, I admit I probably did call him a "black b*****d" and that was a terrible thing to do - I opened my mouth and the words came out without me even realising what I was doing.

When I saw the video I knew I had to do something to say sorry. I spoke to the club secretary Campbell Ogilvie and we released an official statement apologising to everybody who had been offended.

I was ashamed and embarrassed but I was also angry because I felt that people were trying to hang me over this. I had damaged my own reputation but now people were trying to destroy me by labelling me as a racist. I found that very difficult to accept.

If Ikpeba had reacted then I would have understood.

If the referee or Borussia Dortmund had reported me to UEFA and I had been punished then I could have had no complaints.

Even if the German newspapers had made a big issue of it and demanded action be taken against me then I would have had to swallow my medicine.

But no-one in Germany had even noticed or if they did they didn't think it was really such a big deal. Not Ikpeba, not the refree, not the club, not the journalists - no-one.

The only people it seemed I had really upset were those in the Scotish Press and I reached the conclusion that they were working to another agenda.

Maybe I was wrong. Maybe these people really are the world's moral guardians. Maybe they have led the lives of saints and never said something wrong themselves in the heat of the moment. Maybe that's why they were so outraged.

Or maybe they just wanted to use anything they could against me and maybe I had just played straight into their hands.

It went on for days and days until the embarrassment and shame I had felt had turned completely into anger and resentment.

They were interviewing guys like Mark Walters who I remember said that I should be stripped of the captaincy.

I decided then that I would cut off almost all relations with the Press in Scotland because I could not accept this witchhunt against me.

I had done something wrong and I had tried to say sorry for that and to explain that this was a terrible mistake. The only people who couldn't accept that were the people in the newspapers.

I must admit I didn't know what to say to Rod Wallace when all of this was going on but thankfully he knew the truth about me. We were close and he knew that I was no racist.

So he didn't wait for an awkward explanation. He came to me and said: "Listen, don't worry, I know you are not like that."

That was a great gesture from Rod and it made me feel much better about myself. I also remember John Barnes, who was the Celtic manager at that time, gave an interview which really helped the situation.

He tried to explain that when a football player is focused on a game he can say all kinds of different things without meaning a single word. He said that he had come across some racist people in his time but that Lorenzo didn't look like one of them. He said that from everything he knew about me he didn't believe I was a racist guy. It was very good of him.

In fact the next time we played at Celtic Park I saw him in the centre circle during the warm up and I walked over to him to shake his hand and say thank you.

I meant that from the bottom of my heart because John Barnes didn't have to speak up for me.

But clever people know how the game goes and John Barnes is a clever person. He realised I was no racist. He could see I had made a mistake and that I was being made to pay an unfair price.

Evetually it all died down as it always does. The Press moved on to some other target but I still felt uncomfortable for a long time afterwards because I hated the thought of some people seeing me as a racist and I didn't trust the Press after what had been written about me.

Things were bad enough already but it was during this period - just 11 days after that game in Germany - that Advocaat brought our dressing room to the point of revolt.

We were preparing for a trip to Motherwell and, because this had been a turbulent time, there was not a great atmosphere between our dressing room and the Scottish media.

On the Friday John Greig had to get three players to do the usual pre-match Press conferences but none of us wanted to be involved.

Eventually John went to Advocaat to tell him he had a problem and a team meeting was called.

Advocaat stood there in front of us and started barking his orders: "Listen - it is your duty to speak to the Press. If you can't agree who is going to do it then I'll have to decide for you."

He pointed to Barry, Andrei and myself: "You, you and you."

I thought to myself: "Here we go again!" It was time for conflict.

Now, before we go on, I don't want you to think that this was Lorenzo being precious. I realise that taking criticsm is part of my job. If I am not playing well or if the team has suffered a bad result then journalists have every right to have their say. It is what they are paid for, after all.

But, on this occasion, things were not that simple.

I felt I had been badly wronged by the newspapers over the Ikpeba incident - maybe even victimised - and I had taken it all very personally indeed.

Right at that moment it seemed to me that I was the centre of a witchunt and that some people would not be happy until I was stripped of the captaincy - or, better sill, given a ticket back to Bari.

Whether I was right or wrong is not the point here. The point is this is the way I was thinking and I could not face going in there to smile and make small chat with the Press as if nothing had happened between us.

So I stood up and told Advocaat: "No. No way."

And then all hell broke loose.

Advocaat lost control of his anger and started shouting furiously at me in front of the other players. "If you don't do that f****** Press conference then you won't be playing for Rangers tomorrow."

I stuck to my guns. There was no way I was going to be pushed around here or bullied by this little dictator. We stood, toe-to-toe almost, screaming at each other, and then I stormed out of the ground and straight to my car.

I climbed into the driver's seat and phoned my agent to tell him that there was a major problem developing here and that he had better do something about it.

Barry and Andrei came to see me and told me that, to show their support, they would also refuse to do the Press conference. It would be all of us or none of us.

This was a wonderful gesture from them but I told them that this was my battle and that they did not need to get involved.

To be honest, I knew I was now in serious trouble and I didn't see any point in all three of us being left out of the squad for Fir Park. We had a game to win after all.

Arthur Numan then came out to my car and sat with me for a while. Eventually he calmed me down enough for me to realise that I was fighting a battle that I could not win.

So I swallowed my pride and I walked back into the stadium and agreed to do a very, very short interview with the people from the radio.

It was enough to save me from being dropped. So I went to Fir Park, scored my fourth goal of the season there and helped my team mates to a 5-1 win.

We were on course for a league and cup double but, all the while, our dressing room was speeding towards disaster.

The racist episode and it's consequences were bad for me but all you can do is get on with your life and try to live it the right way. I always believed I was a good person and I wasn't going to let all of this ruin my life.

In any case, I had football to play and I knew that I would be back out there at the weekend being called every name under the sun. That's life as a football player. I'm not saying it's right but it happens week in week out.

I wouldn't like to repeat what I have been called. Worse than that is when other players talk badly about my mamma or my girlfriend. It's offensive and there have been many times when I have though to myself: "This is ridiculous," but you don't let it put you off your game.

And I have learned never to hold grudges either because there are a lot of players out there who are completey different people on and off the park. Some guys I know totally transform their personality when they step over that white line.

Some of the most nasty and dangerous people you could ever come across on a football pitch are, in normal life, quiet, nice harmless guys.

My old friend Pasquale Bruno, for example, would do anything for anybody away from football. You could not meet a more funny or friendly guy. But when he got onto that park he was an animal. In fact that was his nickname in Italy - Pasquale Animal - because he made so many bad tackles.

He was one of the most hated men in Serie A. I remember once when Marco van Basten beat him with an unbelievable trick and left Pasquale on the ground. Van Basten went on to score a wonderful goal and then ran back to Pasquale who was still lying on the ground and began doing a samba dance above him.

That's how much Pasquale was hated by the players over there. But he's a good friend of mine and I see him sometimes when I go back to Italy. In fact I saw him just a couple of months ago and I asked him if he'd ever gone out dancing again with Marco van Basten.

He called me a bastard too.

But if there was one guy who I would have to say was the worst for trying to wind people up on the pitch then it has to be my own Ibrox team-mate Billy Dodds.

For one-and-a-half years before he signed for Rangers we had a running feud. Every time we played against each other there would be a fight but we were both clever so neither of us was ever sent off. We knew the game.

We would say things to each other as the game was going on just to try to get a reaction like: "Come on then - let me see what can you can do."

And then, when the referee was not looking, we would try to hit each other too. Actually it got quite heated between us at times.

So I will never forget the December day in that same season that Advocaat bought him and he walked into our dressing room. I could hardly believe my eyes. We just walked up to each other, shook hands and said: "OK, maybe we better stop fighting now."

As it happened Billy was a great success at Rangers that season and his goals helped us to win a second successive league title and also another Scottish Cup.

Five trophies in two years of my captaincy. These should have been happy days but for young Lorenzo things were already taking a turn for the worse.

# Chapter Nine

## DRUGS, BIRDS AND ME

I AM the luckiest guy in the world. I get paid handsomely for doing a job I love. I drive a Ferrari. I live in lovely house and, thankfully, I know how to enjoy myself in the company of a beautiful woman.

One day some years from now I will look back and say that I played my part in the history of one of the greatest clubs in all of Europe.

So, yes, things are good for Lorenzo Amoruso.

They are also good for a lot of people like me - but for some professional football players having everything is not enough.

Perhaps they get greedy. Perhaps they just don't know where to draw the line. Or maybe, no matter what they did for a living, they would be unable to stay away from the evil of drugs.

Thankfully I have never been one of those guys but I have been around long enough to know what goes on in this game and some of it turns my stomach.

When I was a youngster in Italy with Bari I was called in for a dope test after a game against Roma. These tests are commonplace back home - they are conducted after every match whereas in my entire time in Scotland I have been tested only twice.

Anyway, I remember being tested that time along with Angelo Peruzzi, Alessandro Carnevale and Ruggerio Ritzzitelli.

Peruzzi and Carnevale were big, big guys and it turned out that they had been taking a drug to help keep their weight down. I knew something was very wrong because I saw their samples and they were both a very strange colour - almost red.

Now I know strange things can happen naturally. In fact, just to prove it, why don't we try a little experiment here - just you and I. Before you go to bed tonight eat three or four peaches or maybe some asparagus and then check the colour of your urine in the morning. Trust me, you'll be surprised.

But even so - and no matter how much you eat - I can guarantee it won't be red so I knew straight away that these guys were in trouble.

And since then I have been aware of drugs in football even if I have never really understood why anybody would mess with these things.

For starters, no-body can tell me that there is a drug out there which can actually make you become a better football player. OK, maybe they'll make you run faster or feel less tired but if your feet are not good enough then they will never turn you into a player.

That's why, in my sport at least, I don't think there is such a thing as a performance-enhancing drug.

The real problem for football is more to do with the lifestyle of the players away from the pitch.

I have read a lot about these things and so I know that, for example, cocaine only stays in the system for two or three days maximum.

That means a football player can go out after a match, take cocaine that night and still be all clear four or five days later.

So if you are one of the guys who has everything but is always looking for something more then you know you can do these kind of things and still have a very good chance of getting away with it.

I think some players do it. Actually I am sure about it.

But it's not for me and it it never will be. I have never even smoked a cigarette in my life so I suppose I don't know what I am missing.

But I consider myself to be a lucky man. I have the best job in the world and I make a lot of money doing it.

So what do I need with drugs? What happiness could drugs possibly give me that I cannot get from a nice bottle of wine, a good night out with my friends or making love with a beautiful woman?

OK, I know some people have problems in their lives and maybe that is why they would turn to drugs as some kind of last resort - out of desperation.

But why would any football player feel like that? Look, you are talking about people who - if they are feeling low - can simply book up for a weekend away in Paris, London, New York or wherever else they fancy. We are privileged and we should never forget it.

That's the kind of message I would like to get through to the young players these days.

They have an incredible opportunity to live the kind of lives that people all over the world would envy.

But they could lose it all if they are stupid enough to get involved with drugs.

And they also must be very careful with alcohol too. Personally I have made a simple rule which works for me - I do not drink in public places.

If I'm at home or having dinner with friends then, yes, I like a drink. I'm not going to lie to you or make myself out to be some kind of choir boy.

What I am saying is that I will only drink when I know I am somewhere safe. If I am in a nightclub, for example, and some idiot wants to start some trouble - and these things happen - then I know in my mind that I must simply walk away.

But let's say I have had a couple of beers and someone says something very nasty to me. If my mind is not clear then there is a greater chance that I will react and do something stupid.

I can't afford to do that. I have everything to lose. So I don't drink.

But if one or two beers can change the way you react then I wouldn't like to think what kind of damage drugs can do. These are harmful, dangerous chemicals which can change your body and mind forever.

To be honest with you I don't even like taking painkillers. That might sound silly and maybe it is but it's the way I feel and I just wish that more of the new generation felt the same way.

Sometimes I think everything is too easy for the young players of today. They get too much too soon.

When I was a young boy and one of my coaches told me to do something then I did it without asking any questions. I might have disagreed with him but I knew if I said anything then I would be running the risk of a big slap in the face.

I also knew if I went against his wishes then I might ruin my own chances of one day becoming a top professional.

But these days if you try to tell a youngster how to do something there's more chance that he'll turn round and say: "Look, you do your thing and let me live my life my way."

That's not right. A lot has changed in the last 20 years but it's not all been for the better.

Sometimes I imagine what it would be like if I had been born even five years later. In fact, I have talked about it with players the same age as myself and we all agree that our names would be even bigger than they are today.

The fact is the young boys coming into the game now only have to play four or five good games for the top team and they end up with sponsors banging down their doors and massive new contracts from their clubs.

When I was coming through you had to play, play, play, play, play, play, play. Once you had stayed in the first–team for a whole season maybe then you earned a big name. Maybe.

But now a young boy comes in, plays a few games and becomes a big name. Then some club comes in with an offer of £10million only to discover a year later that the boy was not actually good enough in the first place. It's a terrible way to do business but then that is modern-day football.

Sometimes I wonder if the game has gone too far - so far that people have forgotten what it is supposed to be all about.

It seems to me that footballers these days are more like celebrities than athletes.

I know this because I get quite a lot of publicity myself - you might have noticed - and I know that, because of my image, people judge me before they have even met me. They think I am arrogant or that I walk around with my nose in the air and I find that I have to spend a lot of time proving to them that I am, in fact, a different person completely.

Sometimes though, I reach the conclusion that people don't want to know the truth. They have an idea about what kind of guy you are and, for whatever reason, that is the way they want to see you.

And it works both ways because sometimes the rich and famous surround themselves with people who pander to their image. They only want to be told how great they are, how beautiful they are and how talented they are. But they are in trouble when they meet somebody who tells them the truth.

Believe me, I have met a few of these kind of people down the years and they don't tend to like me. In fact they will say Lorenzo is an asshole just because I'm not the kind of guy who will agree with every word they say.

But I am comfortable with myself and I know that I can look at myself in the mirror. I am a good person and I know there are a lot of people who like me because of that - not because of what I may or may not have done on a football pitch.

They are the people in my life that I trust. To be honest, I find it difficult to trust anyone else.

People want to be my friend because I am a famous football player. I told you already about what happened to me in Bari when I found out who my real friends were and maybe that experience has scarred me.

Ever since then I have been aware that people want to be around me just to enjoy the lifestyle. If they are close to me then they know they'll go to the best discos, the best restaurants and the best parties. They can take something away from me.

And so I have learned not to trust anybody - especially girls as there are a lot of gold-diggers out there.

Before I can really start to trust a girl I have to know her for a long time so it is very difficult for me to form loving relationships.

I have to be careful about telling them private things or showing them private things because I don't know what they will do with that information. It is not a nice way to have to live your life because you feel as if you can never really be yourself. You are always trying to hide something about yourself.

But you have to do these things simply to protect yourself.

A few times I have maybe met a girl in a disco or wherever and we might have spent the night together and then I hear that there is a newspaper working on the story.

But if they don't have the pictures or any other kind of proof then there is nothing they can do about it. I have learned that down the years.

But that is why it is so difficult to then go out and meet that girl again. You ask yourself if you are being set up and you worry that if you meet this girl is there going to be some photographer hiding somewhere nearby to get the picture?

The only good thing from my point of view is that I am just a single guy and so it doesn't make such a great scoop if I am seen out on a date. I'm not hurting anybody and I don't understand why people should be so interested in my private life in any case.

OK, I'm a football player but I'm also just a boy who wants to enjoy his life like any other boy of my age.

I don't want to sound big-headed here but do you really think the only reason I can get women is because I play football? I might not be the best-looking boy in the world but I've never had a problem getting girls.

Whatsmore, I have been very fair with every girlfriend I have ever had. If I have been cheating it was only ever at the beginning of the relationship, when you are never sure how things are going to work out, or near the end, when it is clearly not happening or when you are just not sure anymore and so you take a look around to see if you really are in love after all.

But let's not make the mistake of thinking I get more chances with girls just because I'm a football player. I know doctors and lawyers who get just as many women as I do.

OK, I admit it. I'll be in a nightclub and a girl will come up to me and slip her phone number into my pocket. That happens quite often actually.

But it's not just because I'm a football player.

Look, I'll tell you a story here to prove the point.

I was on holiday with my last long-term girlfriend Julie. We had gone for a couple of weeks to Mauritius and the Seychelles.

Anyway, one day Julie wasn't feeling so great so she went back to the room and I went for a long walk on the beach. After ten minutes I met this girl.

We talked for a while, no more than five or ten minutes, and at the end of our conversation she gave me her phone number. She didn't have the first idea who I was.

Anyway, that night I saw her in the hotel and to my astonishment she was sitting with her husband. I had assumed she was a single girl on holiday with her friends.

Of course, I took that piece of paper she had given me and threw it away. There was no point in keeping it.

The point I'm trying to make here is that even if I wasn't a famous football player maybe I would still find it very difficult to trust women.

I have only really had three long-term relationships in my life. My first was with a girl back in Italy, my second was with Cristina who came with me to Scotland, and my third was with Julie.

Maybe that shows that, even when I feel right about a woman, I take a bit longer than most other people do to fall in love.

Sex is different. My best nights of sex have probably been with other girls - none of them my ex-girlfriends.

But you are not only looking for sex from a relationship. Of course, if you can have wonderful sex with your girlfriend then that's great. But you are also looking for something else like personality and brains. Simple things but things that make you enjoy their company.

And, for many reasons, it takes me a lot of time to find out if a girl is actually right for me. Maybe I'm too suspicious.

But at times I must admit I do get lonely. I enjoy my life as a single guy because I can do almost anything I want. I don't have to worry about phoning home every five minutes or making excuses for coming home late. I like that.

But the down side is that most nights I go to bed on my own. I miss the feeling of going to bed with the woman I love, wakening up next to her in the morning, going for walks, preparing meals together and eating out. I even miss the feeling of going shopping for groceries together - I have no-one to share these simple moments with and that can be difficult.

It would be nice sometimes just to be able to sit there at night and express my sentiments to someone who I know wants to listen. I have to keep these thoughts to myself - or share them with the four walls of my living room.

And then of course, there is the question of kids. I love kids and one day I want to be a father but before I bring a new life into this world I must be completely and utterly sure that I have found the right wife.

I need to find a woman who I know loves me, understands me and wants to be a part of my life. I will have to be more than 100 per cent sure because three years down the line I don't want my kids to be split between two different houses.

Divorce is a terrible thing for any child to have to go through and I don't want to be responsible for making my own children suffer something like that or have to watch their mother and father fighting and falling apart.

The older I get the higher my standards rise and the more demanding I become with women. Basically I am looking for the prefect women. The one who will fix my life up 100 per cent. It's going to be tough to find that woman and I have come to accept that.

I also have to wonder if I may have to finish playing football first before I can find my true love.

I know myself and I know I find it almost impossible to have a long distance relationship. If we are apart for too long then I know for sure that I will cheat on her. But that's just because I'm a boy and we boys just can't go a month or two months without sex.

Two or three weeks I can just about handle but after a month it becomes very difficult.

I met a girl back in Italy recently and I am still in touch with her but I know it's going to be difficult for me to stay faithful if she stays over there while I am on my own over here.

This was the main reason behind my split with Cristina. The wedding was planned. There was just one year to go.

But she didn't like living in Scotland and that became more and more of a strain on our relationship.

She was quite a big fashion model in Italy so when she came to Glasgow to live with me I found her an agency so she could continue to work. But the money models make in Glasgow is not really anything near what they can earn in places like Milan. That was the first problem but I told her not to worry about money because I would pay for everything - it was my responsibility to look after her.

But looking back it was never going to work. She didn't speak very good English - she would let me do all the talking and that wasn't a very nice thing to do. I believe if you move to a new country you should make an effort to blend in and to learn the language.

So I sent her to college for three-and-a-half months but even then her heart did not seem to be in it.

I'm not saying I was perfect. As we have discussed already I had some issues of my own over this period but I was not about to leave my job just to find an easy solution to our problems.

I had to get through these problems because I had to protect my career. Football players can only make money for a short time before they have to hang up their boots.

That means I have to make a lot sacrifices and these also affect my relationships.

If you want to be with me then you have to realise we can't go out on Friday nights and most Saturday nights as well. We can't go on holiday when we want. We can't drink when we want and we can't disappear back to Italy when it suits us.

Cristina couldn't cope with all of these sacrifices and I can't really blame her for that.

But it was a bad time in my life. I had already fallen out with Advocaat and I needed another operation on my ankle which would keep me out of the Scottish Cup Final against Aberdeen.

Maybe I should have been more considerate but at that time I could only see my own problems. I admit I was being selfish.

But this really was a terrible time for me and things got even worse the day after I went under the knife. I was lying in my hospital bed when I got a phone call from a journalist telling me that Advocaat was secretly trying to sell me to Sunderland. What?

I could not believe my ears. How dare he?

Suddenly my head was swirling with all kinds of negative thoughts and for a long time afterwards I was stressed out and I wasn't myself. It was Cristina who suffered.

Then one day she started to moan at me so I got in the car and took off. I just needed some space.

When I came back she was upset and angry and told me that I had no right to leave her when she wasn't feeling well. Women, at times like this, can be crazy you know.

But the truth was everything was falling apart. My career was in turmoil, my club no longer wanted me and my manager didn't even have the decency to tell me to my face.

Now my relationship was on the rocks. Everything in my life was falling apart.

Soon after that she went back to Italy. We tried to patch things up over the phone and she told me a few times that she was coming back to Scotland to live with me.

But she never did.

Then came the final hammer blow when she phoned me to tell me that she was seeing another boy back in Italy. If I had been upset before then I was shattered by this news.

All along I think I had been telling myself that we would get through this eventually. Yes, she was the one.

But I knew now for sure that it was over and it hit me straight between the eyes.

As a matter of fact she had phoned me to drop this bombshell on the day before our first Old Firm game of the season against Celtic and their new manager Martin O'Neill.

I remember I was at the team hotel at the time and that day I was also on the phone to my mum a lot because she was unwell back in Bari.

Actually I had two conversations going at the same time on

two different phones - one with my mum and the other with Cristina.

As my fianceé was telling me about the new man in her life I felt my heart tear and my head begin to spin. And in less than 24 hours time I had to play in a Glasgow derby.

I went down for dinner that night with my team-mates and all of a sudden I was overcome with emotion. I started to cry at the table in front of them.

I got up and went to the toilet for five minutes to get my head together. When I came back everyone was concerned and they were asking me what had happened.

I just pretended everything was OK and I finished my meal but these guys weren't stupid and so, when I went back to my room, there was a knock at my door. It was the team doctor Gert Jan Goudswaard.

He wanted to make sure I was OK and then Sergio arrived too asking if there was anything he could do. We had a good chat and by the end of it I felt a little bit better but it was a long, long night.

Let's just say I was not in the best frame of mind going into the game at Parkhead and within ten minutes of kick-off we found ourselves 3-0 down and crashing hopelessly towards a 6-2 defeat. I was in a state of turmoil.

It took me four or five months to recover mentally and emotionally from this but even then I don't really believe that time heals.

When you are hurt this badly it leaves a scar forever. Maybe one year later it isn't painful to the touch but you only have to look at it to remember exactly how this mark was made.

I was scarred by what had happened just the same way as I had been scarred that day in Advocaat's office when he told me the armband was no longer mine.

I suppose it is just as well for me then that I like to have challenges in all aspects of my life.

When you go through episodes like these and you survive them and come out the other side still smiling then you realise that there isn't really any more that life can throw at you.

You just have to stay strong and wait for your moment to come again. If you allow yourself to wallow in a pool of self-pity then you drown. It's as simple as that.

Maybe it is experiences like these which have given me such a strange character. I know that sometimes I can be downright nasty and I don't like myself when I behave in this way.

But maybe that is when my survival instincts kick in.

And - back at Ibrox - I was about to rely on these instincts more than ever before.

# *Chapter Ten*

## MY NIGHTMARE BEGINS

WELCOME to the most bleak and distressing period of my life. You are about to witness me hitting rock bottom.

But before we explore this terrible episode let me set the scene for you and take you back to the night we won our second championship under Advocaat.

As you may recall we were playing against St Johnstone in Perth in a Sunday evening match the day after Celtic had more or less handed us the title by dropping points at home.

We knew the league was ours but we still put on a good performance with Billy Dodds scoring a couple of good goals.

The reason I bring this up is because recently Advocaat

accused of us of not wanting to celebrate this triumph properly with our own supporters. He said he had to push us out onto the park afterwards and he believed this was a sign that we had lost our hunger for silverware.

This, he says, was his reason for imposing even more rules upon the team in our third season together - and it was that decision which I believe brought our dressing room to the point of collapse.

So I think you deserve an explanation.

We'll start with a confession - Advocaat had a point. We didn't see the need for a big celebration because we all knew the league had been over for months. Celtic were so far behind us that season it was only ever a question of when we would win it, not if.

And the fact that Celtic had slipped up again just 24 hours earlier really took the edge off our night. I'm sure you will agree the best parties are always spontaneous but there was not even the slightest element of surprise about this one.

It was also a dreadful night – freezing cold and pouring rain – so, yes, it is fair to say that we were not in a state of euphoria and some of the guys were simply looking forward to getting on the bus and going home.

But Advocaat was correct to tell us to get back out there because we owed it to the supporters who had travelled to Perth to give them something to remember.

I remember I came out carrying this massive bottle of champagne - it was so heavy I will never forget it - and I sprayed it everywhere.

We went on a lap of honour and we enjoyed ourselves. After all we had won a league and this was our moment with the fans. In that respect Advocaat was absolutely right. In fact he's like me because he realises that winning trophies is everything.

But from that moment on, until only very recently in fact, we did not see eye to eye again.

I was carrying an injury at the time from a previous visit to McDiarmid Park when Craig Moore and myself collided trying to clear a throw in inside our own box. I shouted for him to leave it but he didn't hear me and so he put his foot in as I was making contact with the ball and then my ankle cracked against his studs.

Three or four days later a scan showed that a piece of cartilage had been chipped off and so I went back to Italy to see my old friend Dr Maertens who was in the country at that time.

He told me if I could suffer the pain then I could keep on playing for two or three months but that eventually I would need to have an operation.

We had a lot of games still to play - two of them against Celtic - so I had a meeting with Advocaat and the club doctor and we decided that I should delay the surgery for as long as possible.

It was sore, believe me, but the team needed me and I was happy to play my part.

But before the end of the season I knew I couldn't keep going and I realised it was more important for me to get the operation done so that I would be fit in time for the start of the next campaign and the Champions League qualifiers.

And that's when it all started going wrong.

I knew I would have to miss out on the Scottish Cup Final against Aberdeen and that was a huge personal disappointment but, again, we had to think about what was best for the team.

So I went under the knife in Belgium on the 10th of May.

Now I should also point out here that, away from football, things were not going well either as I was having a lot of trouble keeping my relationship with my fiancée Cristina together.

We have spoken about this period in my life already of course but, in case you weren't paying attention, we broke up in the April of that year.

It had a bad effect on me both on and off the park as I believe if the personal side of your life is causing you problems then the professional side suffers and vice versa.

So let's just say I had a lot on my mind the day Dr Maertens cut me open.

But the following day, while I was still recuperating in hospital in Antwerp, I received the telephone call which brought me to the point of walking away from Rangers for good. OK, hobbling away.

It was a journalist who hit me with the news. Advocaat had sold me to Sunderland behind my back. I could not believe what I was hearing.

The guy asked what I knew about it and I gave him a straight answer: "F**k all."

Within five minutes the phone was ringing again. This time it was a girl who worked for the Rangers News.

She asked how I was and what I thought about the news that Sunderland had agreed a fee for me. I told her I was upset about it and that I felt I had been badly let down by the club.

I should have thought twice but I was too angry. Instead, I just told her: "When a club needs you they give you everything - when they think they don't need you any more they kick you in the ass."

Well, this caused quite a stir back home in Glasgow and it meant everything was out in the open by the time I returned to cover the Scottish Cup Final as a studio guest with the BBC at Hampden.

It was a difficult day for me because this was also the day that the Rangers supporters wore orange tops in honour of our Dutch manager.

I can't pretend I was happy to see him being honoured in this way - not when he was showing me such disrespect.

I watched my team mates lift the trophy and I was happy for them but deep down I couldn't really enjoy the occasion. After the game I went straight to Ibrox for the team celebration. But I was in no mood for a party.

Instead, I went to the manager's office before it all began to have it out with him in person.

I raged: "What the f**k is the story here? You have sold me to Sunderland?"

He said: "Look Lorenzo, this is how football goes. The clubs get together and make a deal and then it is up to the player to decide if he wants to make the move or not."

But I said: "Listen, maybe you treat animals like that but you should not treat people in this way. All you had to do was phone me to let me know what was going on. Is that too much to ask? This is my career you are playing with."

I was furious. I could not believe the matter-of-fact way he was talking about the decision to turn my life upside down. I had given my blood, sweat and tears to help him build a new team for Rangers. He had asked me for my help and I had given him everything.

My God, I had been playing on for months in agony because I was thinking about what was best for Rangers. And all that time Rangers - or Advocaat - had been thinking about selling me.

And now here he was treating me with utter contempt.

I kept thinking back to that phone call I had received in the hospital and it made me angrier and angrier. "All I am asking is that you show me some respect," I repeated.

But respect is not a word which is in Advocaat's dictionary. In my book it doesn't matter if you are a waitress or the President of the United States - you deserve to be treated with respect.

That is the way I live my life because I know that there will be times when things go against you and that is when you rely on people to help you out. If you have treated them badly in the past then why should they come to your assistance?

But now I was being hung out to dry by Advocaat and I have to say I felt let down by a lot of people. I did not receive any calls of support from certain quarters which surprised me.

What did come, though, was the call from Sunderland asking me to travel there for talks with Peter Reid and so, knowing that Rangers didn't want me, I decided to look out for number one.

I went to see Reid and I also had talks with the vice-chairman. I was there for half a day and they offered me a very good contract but, and I might as well be honest here, it was not good enough to make me want to live in a place like Sunderland.

I saw enough that day to know that I couldn't enjoy living there the way I enjoy living in Glasgow.

Also, there would be no Champions League and no UEFA Cup to look forward to. OK, I had a look around and I admit it was a wonderful stadium. I'm told they have a great support as well.

But I weighed everything up and I felt there was no way this team was going to make it into the top five or six in the Premiership. They told me they had big plans but I was not convinced.

So the only reason left was the money and I admit if they had met my demands then you probably wouldn't be reading this book right now. But they said I was looking for too much and so the transfer collapsed.

They had offered me an extra £150,000 a year to move but I didn't see that as a good enough reason. I was giving up too much in terms of the lifestyle I enjoyed in Glasgow, the friends I had made there and, of course, European football.

For me £150,000 didn't come close to compensating me for what they were asking me to leave behind. I know some people will read this and they'll probably be disgusted that I'm talking as if £150,000 is an insignificant amount of money. Other people might think I'm nuts. But, the truth is, it really didn't make that big a difference.

So I said no and then I returned to Italy to continue my rehabilitation. They phoned me again and asked me to come back for more talks. I agreed but the sums still did not add up so I decided I would go back to Ibrox - for the time being at least.

But Advocaat had also been busy that summer. He had bought Bert Konterman and this was a big, big problem.

When I arrived back in Glasgow after completing my rehabilitation everyone was telling me that I would be a fringe player. The best I could hope for was a seat on the bench.

I had already had a couple of phone calls from the chairman and the manager to tell me that Bert would be starting the season in my position but my answer was a simple one: "I'm coming back to fight for my place - I've never been scared of a fight."

I surprised them by coming back in great shape ten days before the beginning of the league. Nobody had expected this.

But it was just as well I was ready because Craig Moore was injured now and so I was back in the team for our opening game against St Johnstone - and I was still wearing my armband.

Now this was a big issue for me because I was beginning to suspect that there was a plan to strip me of the captaincy.

The bridge between myself and my manager had been broken and, even although he told the Press he was happy to have me back at the club, I had an idea of what he was trying to do to me.

Let's be blunt - he tried to stab me in the back and now I felt I could no longer trust this man.

But there was only one response I could give and that was to work harder than ever before to stay in the team.

Things went well for a while, so well that the spotlight was drifting away from Lorenzo and onto other players in the team. Bert and Fernando Ricksen had been signed in the summer and they were having some problems of their own adjusting to life at Ibrox and to Scottish football in particular.

We were still winning games but the truth was we were struggling to gel and the results were coming in spite of our new-look defence rather than because of it.

In that opening game against St Johnstone we went 1-0 down before coming back to win it 2-1. At Kilmarnock we went 2-0 down and then fought back to win it 4-2.

Something was going badly wrong and we knew it.

I'm not saying this was all down to Bert and Fernando. Of course it wasn't, but they were not settling in properly all the same. Fernando was very nervous, even in training, and Bert was having problems understanding our system.

We had gone from having the strongest defence in the league when we won the title - I think we had only lost 10 goals all season - to having one of the weakest. That says enough.

But we kept it going until the first Old Firm game of the season when the wheels came crashing off at Celtic Park.

I have told you already about what went on before that match when Cristina phoned me at the team hotel to tell me she had found herself a new man. So you know my state of mind going into that game.

But, even so, I can't just blame myself for that 6-2 defeat. I have watched the game a few times on video and I know I can't claim to have played well. But I know I wasn't the worst player in a blue shirt that day.

Anyway, that game was really the beginning of the end for this team of ours and the sign that the balance of power was moving from the south side of Glasgow to the city's east end.

We fell five points behind Celtic soon after when we drew 1-1 at Dens Park and this one really was all my fault.

I made a terrible mistake on the edge of my own box which allowed Juan Sara to score the equaliser. I knew I was to blame and I held my hands up in the dressing room after the game.

I apologised in front of my team-mates and the manager and admitted that, because of me, we had dropped two points.

But, as I spoke, I could feel that something was terribly wrong. I could tell then - for the first time - that I was on my own in that dressing room.

Nobody said a word to me or tried to comfort me. That was not so bad because I had never asked for anyone's help before and I didn't need it then either. But what it did show me was that we were losing our unity as a team and that spelled disaster.

Looking back upon this period I have to say I think everybody was starting to feel lonely - we were drifting apart.

There were now eight Dutchmen in that dressing room - Giovanni van Bronkhurst, Arthur Numan, Michael Mols, Bert Konterman and Fernando Ricksen as well as Advocaat, Bert Van Lingen and the team doctor Gert Jan Goudswaard - and the rest of us seemed to be on the outside looking in.

It was the same as Louis van Gaal surrounding himself with Dutch players in Spain. I remember thinking: "This is Barcelona II here."

There was not a great deal of happiness around the club and Advocaat helped to make sure of that by introducing new rules, more strict than ever before.

After two years of winning almost everything and doing well

in Europe I believe this was the time for him to relax and give the players a little more freedom. Instead, he went the other way.

For example, on one occasion my parents were coming to visit me and I had promised to pick them up at Glasgow Airport. This was really important to me because I had not seen them in a long time and having gone through some bad times I was really looking forward to seeing them.

I asked Advocaat if it would be OK for me to be excused from eating with the team so that I could be there to meet them off the plane. He shook his head and told me to book them a taxi.

And it wasn't just me. Some of the other guys had the same problem when their wives or girlfriends came over and they were told the same thing.

These kind of things caused resentment to build up and contributed to the problems we had with the spirit in the camp.

And all the time the Dutch influence was becoming more and more evident. They would talk Dutch in the dressing room and I found that unacceptable - especially as I had always made sure that all the Italians had used English to communicate in front of the other players.

Even during games sometimes Advocaat would shout orders in Dutch – it was becoming ridiculous.

Don't get me wrong - I'm sure he was doing it for the right reasons and that it was just easier for him to explain his tactics to the other Dutch guys in this way. At least I hope that's what he was doing.

I felt that the rest of us were being excluded. Even if we didn't agree with what he was saying we should have at least been given the chance to understand it.

But there was nothing we could do about it because our opinions simply didn't count. It was like throwing a glass of water into the sea.

So things were getting worse all the time and the situation became critical in October when we lost three league games in a row against St Johnstone, Hibs and Kilmarnock.

Up until that point we had managed to paper over the cracks – especially with our first two performances in the Champions League when we destroyed Sturm Graz at Ibrox 5-0 and then won 1-0 away to Monaco.

After Monte Carlo we headed back to Perth where we played a very bad game. There was no commitment - we were a collection of individuals rather than a team.

I remember during that game I snapped at Neil McCann for giving the ball away at St Johnstone's second goal. He tried a piece of skill but Momo Sylla saw it coming, robbed him, drove forward for ten metres without anybody chasing him and then fired a great shot to make it 2-1.

My blood was boiling and I lost control. I shouted at Neil: "What the f**k are you doing?"

I knew it was the wrong thing to do but I couldn't help myself. I was so angry at the way things were going.

Neil was quite rightly upset with me but after a couple of days I took him aside on the training ground and apologised.

Of all people I should have known better because accidents like this can happen to anybody. After all, I had made a costly mistake of my own at Dundee and Neil hadn't shouted at me that day.

So I knew I was in the wrong and that's why I said sorry. But I only mention this to let you see the way things were going inside our camp.

Advocaat's response to that defeat was to slaughter us in the newspapers for the first time ever, calling us big heads.

Of course, he was trying to get some kind of reaction but the team was now too fragmented to fight back and we stumbled from one bad result to the next like a drunk on a Saturday night.

In the middle of this mess we had to go to Austria to play Sturm Graz knowing a win would give us 10 points and put us within touching distance of the second phase of the Champions League. It was a shocking night.

Advocaat got the system all wrong and forced Giovanni to play when we all knew he was not even a photo-copy of his true self. It was completely out of order for the manager to do this.

Advocaat went for three at the back - myself on the right as a man marker, Sergio Porrini in the middle as a sweeper and Bert man marking on the left.

Now I'm not saying for a second that I could be as good a manager as Advocaat - not yet anyway - but I knew that he had got it all wrong that night.

If he wanted us to play like that then it would have made much more sense to do what we had done a year earlier in Parma when Sergio and I were the markers.

Better still, he could have gone with a flat back four because we knew we weren't playing well at the time and all we had to do was keep it secure in defence, soak up everything Sturm Graz could throw at us and then try to hit them on the counter attack.

But Advocaat went for broke. I think he played with five strikers that night believing we would go there and beat them the way we had done at Ibrox.

He should have shown them more respect because they were a completely different team at home - as they had proved already by beating Monaco and Galatasaray there.

The whole thing was a disaster and we lost 2-0.

By the time we faced Kilmarnock at Ibrox we were on our

knees. They destroyed us 3-0 in front of our supporters and I remember the fans turned against me in particular.

The following Monday I decided I had to speak to the manager about what was going wrong with this team of ours. It was time to get everything out in the open because we could not allow this to continue.

But what I didn't realise was that Advocaat had a few ideas of his own and he was about to let me in on them.

And this brings us back to where we started our story. Back to the manager's office at the top of that famous marble staircase. Back to the day he tried to rip my heart out.

This was an attack on my character and on my professional reputation. Let's be clear - he was admitting to the world that Rangers had big problems but that one person, Lorenzo Amoruso, was to blame for them all.

You know it's funny but as the bottom was falling out of our world I cannot recall Advocaat once standing up and taking any kind of responsibility. Not once.

I know I was not playing well and I was big enough to say so. But there were 10 other players out there and I was not losing games all on my own.

Just try for a moment to imagine the pressure I was feeling when we faced Monaco at home in the last group game needing a win to go through. Everyone was looking at me and pointing accusing fingers in my direction and I knew before we played that game that, if we lost and went out of Europe, it would all be pinned on me.

So you will have an idea of how I was feeling when, near the end of the match, with us defending a 2-1 lead, I lost possession and saw Marco Simeone running in on goal.

Yes, I had made a mistake but this was not a repeat of what had happened at Dundee a few weeks earlier. This time I was 50 yards away from my own goal when I lost the ball.

There was plenty of time for us to recover and to defend the situation properly as a team but then, like I say, we were no longer a proper team. What happened next painted the perfect picture of what had gone wrong in our dressing room.

We had lost the desire to fight for each other and to help each other out.

No-one chased back as Simeone went through. It was as if nobody saw it as their responsibility. This was Lorenzo's mess and it was up to him to get us out of it.

But I could only watch in horror as Simeone pulled the trigger. Even then his shot was right in the middle of the goal but Jesper Christiansen let it go straight through him. To this day I don't know what Jesper was thinking about.

What I did know was that I was on my own now more than ever before.

Again nothing much was said in the dressing room but the next morning I saw the papers and realised that Michael and Arthur had blamed me for our exit.

I have told you about what happened on the training ground between Arthur and myself and I should point out also that this is all very much in the past now as far as both of us are concerned. There are absolutely no problems between us now.

But these were difficult times for everybody and it was during this period that there was another training ground bust up involving Andrei Kanchelskis and Fernando Ricksen - and this one really was the real thing.

The stupid thing is that Andrei and Fernando are two of the nicest guys you could ever meet but you would not have thought so that day as the punches started to fly.

I'm sure Fernando will admit himself that his character changes when he pulls on his boots. Sometimes he can be a bit nasty – even on the training ground.

And on this particular day the atmosphere was already very tense. Andrei was unhappy because he was being frozen out of the team by Advocaat at the time and maybe that's why he reacted so angrily to one of Fernando's challenges.

It quickly escalated into a full blown fight - punching, kicking, the works. They were serious and they were trying to hurt each other.

We jumped in to separate the pair of them and once it had all calmed down Advocaat marched over and ordered Andrei to get onto the bus and get back to Ibrox. Fernando was allowed to stay.

I could not stand by and say nothing. Things were now getting totally out of hand. He could not send one of them away and let the other carry on as if nothing had happened. This was blatant favouritism and it could not be tolerated.

But it was not just me who felt like this. For the first time ever the players united against Advocaat's decision and told him this was not right. Myself, Sergio, Jorg, Arthur and a few of the other lads all told him he should either send both of them back to Ibrox or let both of them stay and finish training.

He backed down. He just walked away and let Van Lingen take charge for the rest of the session.

By the way, within a couple of minutes Fernando and Andrei were the best of friends again but this was a moment which would live with me forever because it was the first and only time that as players we had made the decision instead of Advocaat.

I'm sure he realised later that he was being stupid because he didn't take any further action other than giving both players the fines which, of course, they deserved.

News of this fight was not slow in hitting the back pages and then everyone began to speculate on the divisions inside our dressing room. Our problems had gone public in the worst possible way.

Suddenly everyone had an opinion on what was going wrong at Ibrox and the common belief was that we were now all at each other's throats on a daily basis. That was never the case.

In any business, if you put 26 guys together then they will not all be best friends. But there were no real rifts between us.

Having said that things had definitely changed between us because we were not socialising together the way we had at the start.

In our first two seasons together we would go out for a meal together at least once a week - myself, Sergio, Giovanni, Jorg, Claudio Reyna, Rod Wallace, Tony Vidmar, Gabby Amato, Andrei and sometimes Arthur as well.

It was a very good group. OK, so we may not have drunk the way the nine-in-a-row team did but these were good times all the same and there was a strong spirit between us.

But in that third season the atmosphere changed because the Dutch colony had taken control and the rest of us felt like outsiders.

I'll give you one stupid story as an example.

Right at the start of the season, when I had come back from Italy after recovering from my operation, I told the doctor I was in great shape and that I was ready to play.

He couldn't believe it and said he wanted to put me through a fitness test with a couple of the Dutch players who had also come back late after playing for Holland at Euro 2000.

So myself, Giovanni and Bert were given what they call a beep test.

Now this is hard work. It involves running from one cone to another over the space of 20 metres. The doctor plays a tape on the stereo and every time it beeps you have to be on a cone. As the tape goes on so the speed of the beeps increase until you can't keep up any more.

But there is also a voice on the tape which gives you instructions as you are running. And yes, you've guessed it, the voice on our tape was speaking in Dutch.

I remember they used the same tape again at the end of the season to check the condition of everyone in the squad. It was unbelievable. We had to keep asking the Dutch guys to translate so we knew what we were doing. Chaos, absolute chaos.

These are the kind of things I'm talking about when I say we were made to feel like outsiders. It was a sign of the direction the club was moving in and small things like this created the bad atmosphere in our dressing room.

It was clear to me that we had too many Dutchmen. I have nothing against Dutch people - it's just that I believe this great club was becoming more about Holland than Scotland and that can't be right.

If you remember, part of the reason I was able to settle here was because I had come to Scotland with an open mind, ready and willing to embrace the culture and to make whatever changes were needed for me to fit in.

But now Ibrox was like a little piece of the Netherlands. It was a strange, strange time to be a Rangers player.

Suddenly the very guys who had done so much to help us win five trophies out of six, were being treated like dirt - guys like Neil McCann, Andrei and even Doddsy who had been our top scorer.

They couldn't get near the team anymore and Rod Wallace, who was probably the best finisher at the club, was another victim. I know that Rod didn't like the manager and he was made to pay a heavy price.

At the end of season they made him an offer to stay at the

club because they realised we had problems up front but by then Rod had had enough and he took the decision to leave on a Bosman.

Yes, things were changing all right. Celtic were now moving away from us at the top of the league under new manager Martin O'Neill.

And you know the most annoying thing of all? To this day I am convinced that we had the players to win the title again that season. People talk about how strong Celtic became under O'Neill but I don't see it that way - it was more a matter of how weak Rangers had become. Celtic didn't win that title, we gave it away.

I know I will be accused of sour grapes here but there is no way Celtic were better than us, even if they won the title easily in the end. They were stronger physically but we had the more talented individuals. And that was our problem. We were a team of individuals while Celtic were running, fighting and scratching for each other. Their team spirit was soaring while ours was falling apart.

If I'm being really honest then, when I look back upon this period, I have to say it was as if nobody gave a f**k what happened during the games.

You're a defender, I'm a striker. You do your job, I'll do mine.

Nobody tried to bring it all together and that is the worst thing that can happen to any team.

It doesn't matter how good your players are – if they are not fighting for one another then your team isn't worth anything.

That was why we were hammered 6-2 at Celtic Park in August. That's why we lost three games in a row in October. That's why we allowed very average sides like Sturm Graz and Galatasaray to knock us out of Europe. Scrub that, they were not even average. Galatasaray were terrible - even worse than Sturm Graz.

They played with just one player, Jardel, up front and with Hagi, who must have been about 52-years-old by then, playing behind him.

But, for some reason, when they came to Glasgow we played with four defenders against them and as a result we created just one chance of our own all night - a Neil McCann header - and we drew 0-0.

Our confidence was gone and as the season went on and we got worse and worse. It felt as if our soul was being destroyed. Nobody could do anything to stop the rot.

We brought in Tore Andre Flo for £12 million in November and he scored on his debut against Celtic. I scored that day as well and we won 5-1. It was maybe the last time we enjoyed ourselves that season.

We worked as a unit that day too and I honestly believe we could have scored nine or 10 goals. I wish we had.

At the time I thought it might even be my last ever Glasgow derby because I was now completely miserable and I had decided enough was enough. It was time for me to get myself out of Ibrox.

After losing my armband I had told my agent to find me a new club and round about Christmas West Ham came in for me. I got a phone call from Harry Redknapp. He told me he was interested in buying me and that he knew things weren't going well for me with Rangers.

I said: "OK, no problem. I'm coming."

To be honest this was what I had been waiting for. Or so I thought.

But looking back perhaps there were some people who knew more about Lorenzo than Lorenzo himself.

I'm talking about guys like Richard Gough, Ally McCoist, Andy Goram, Ian Durrant and John Brown.

These men were the heroes of nine-in-a-row and they were the people I turned to when I needed advice. They said to me they didn't know how I could play for Advocaat again after everything that had happened with Sunderland and then the captaincy.

At that time I had convinced myself I was only playing for Rangers to win myself a transfer. But these guys could see something in me that even I could not.

Every single one of them said exactly the same thing. They told me they would not have stood for this themselves and they said that the fact that I was still out there pulling on a blue jersey proved that I must really love this club.

They could see it because they too knew what it meant to fall in love with Glasgow Rangers. I maybe didn't know it at the time but I had fallen head over heels also.

And that's why these problems I was experiencing were hurting me so badly. That was why I could no longer stay. I loved Rangers but the club didn't feel the same way about me - and that was slowly destroying me.

So I told Redknapp to get my transfer fee sorted out with Rangers. I decided I had to cut all ties.

I went back to Florence during the winter break where I met with Redknapp and his vice-chairman. Everything was perfect. We left each other believing that, in a matter of days, I would be a West Ham player.

The last game before the shut-down had been against St Mirren and I honestly thought that would be my last match as a Rangers player. But, not for the first time in my life, fate was about to step in and take control.

Redknapp parted company with West Ham and the transfer collapsed. Even if I was not happy about it at the time, my Rangers career had been saved from death row.

I may not have known it but this was one of best things that ever happened to me.

Maybe I would have been happy at West Ham. In fact, maybe I actually needed to change club because of all the things that had been said and done against me.

I had never quit anything in my life or walked away from any fight but this was different. I was disgusted with the treatment I was receiving.

But now I was left with no choice but to stay in Glasgow, work through these problems, and continue playing under Advocaat.

Thankfully my relationship with the supporters was improving after some really rocky times earlier in the season. They could see that I was giving them everything and that even if the team was not playing well I would never hide.

I remember when I signed for Rangers the first thing I said to David Murray. When he asked me: "What can you give this club?"

I said: "Listen, I don't know if I can make this club any better than it is already. The only promise I can make is that every time Lorenzo plays for Rangers he will finish the game with his shirt soaked in sweat."

So I decided to stick to that promise and I think the fans were the first to realise how hard I was prepared to work to turn things around. Sure, I had played some bad games – but they could see I was one of the few players who was giving more than 100 per cent and at least trying to do something about this terrible situation that we faced on the pitch.

And yet we were only nine points behind Celtic that winter. Even though we were in a state of turmoil I really believed we could still catch them.

But in the last five minutes of the very last training session of the winter break I tore a muscle and ended up back on the sidelines. I think the expression is Lucky White Heather?

I missed two games against Celtic - the first at Hampden in the CIS Cup. We lost it 3-1.

Then I missed a league match at Parkhead which we lost 1-0.

And that was our season over. We had just one trophy left to go for, the Scottish Cup, and we were starting to play a little bit better.

But, in fact, we were just saving our worst for that quarter-final tie against Dundee United. Now I had been through quite a lot that season.

But this was the lowest point of them all. I remember that game as if we had played it last night. We did not create one single chance in 90 minutes. Not even a shot on goal. We were absolutely and utterly hopeless. It was the worst game I have ever been involved in as a Rangers player - yes, and that does include that 6-2 game at Celtic Park.

So that was it. Season over.

After two seasons of sweeping all before us we were now being brushed away like rubbish in the street. The party was over and I remember thinking: "So what happens now?"

Everybody was thinking about their own business now. It was every man for himself.

All we knew for certain was that this team of ours was in big, big trouble and we couldn't see a way out.

Throughout all of this time I had decided not to do anything with the Press but before I left for Italy that summer I agreed, as a favour for a friend, to do an interview with some small television station in Lanarkshire. I had never even heard of it before so I didn't think it would make big news. I could not have been more wrong.

This was the first time I had admitted that I wanted out. I said

I wanted to finish the season and that then I would go away for good. I had had enough and my relationship with the manager was now so bad that we could not go on this way any longer.

I was serious too. This time there really would be no going back.

# *Chapter Eleven*

## THE LONG GOODBYE

IT HAD been a season of tears and tantrums but the saddest day came when we finished our dismal league campaign with a game against Hibs at Ibrox.

I had made up my mind that this would be my last game. Again.

But this time I was not alone. My good friend Jorg Albertz and Tugay had also had enough. In fact Jorg had been telling me about it for a few weeks. He knew that Hamburg were in for him and it was only a matter of them agreeing a fee with Rangers. Knowing the way Advocaat felt about him we did not expect that to be a problem. So I knew he was leaving and the fans knew it too.

I ran out onto the pitch that day to see flags and banners all over the stadium begging Jorg and myself not to leave. "We love you both," they said, "You will always be in our hearts".

And from that moment on I knew it would be an emotional day. I played that game with a lump in my throat the size of a Mitre Five.

I had come through a lot with these supporters. Good times and bad.

My God, it had only been a few short months ago that they were booing me as my world was falling apart.

But they had been there to celebrate with me also when I was lifting trophies and, throughout all of these experiences, a strong bond had grown between us. Perhaps none of us really realised how strong until it looked as if our relationship was at an end.

I must admit I was shocked with this response. Usually football is about the team - the way it should be. But this was all very personal and suddenly I could see for myself that these people really loved me. Maybe, somewhere deep inside, I was realising that I really loved them too. It was just like Richard Gough and the others had said.

But I had made my decision and I was going to stick to it. In any case, my problem was with Advocaat and I didn't see him holding up any banners in the dugout.

So I decided I just wanted to get this over and done with. I tried not to think too much about the supporters and their messages. It was too upsetting. I had to be strong.

And when it was all over I didn't even hang around at the end to say my goodbyes. I'm still not sure exactly why but I ran straight up the tunnel while Jorg and Tugay went on a lap of honour.

I honestly don't know what I was scared of. Maybe it was because Jorg and Tugay had both sorted out their new contracts by then with Hamburg and Blackburn. I, on the other hand, did not have anything sorted out although I knew that Lazio were now showing a lot of interest.

Maybe I didn't want to make a fuss because this was difficult enough.

Or maybe in my heart of hearts I was just scared of saying goodbye to this club and to these supporters.

I don't know what it was. I just remember feeling awful.

I sat in the dressing room at the end of it all and I felt as if my body was empty. I was completely drained. And then I saw Jorg and Tugay come in. They had lost it.

They were crying on each other's shoulders because this was not what they wanted. I saw how much they were hurting and, for the first time, I started to ask myself if I was making the right decision.

I knew why Jorg was going. He had told me often enough. He couldn't share a dressing room with Advocaat any longer only to be given 10 or 15 minutes in the team as a substitute. He didn't want to spend his entire week hoping that one of his friends would get injured just so that he could get a place in the team.

Jorg was too good to be treated like this. He was now being offered a chance to go back to Germany, back to his family and friends and play there week in, week out.

But it was breaking his heart. This was one of the saddest sights I had ever seen inside our dressing room and I suppose I had to ask myself if I was strong enough to make the same decision.

The chairman had phoned me a couple of weeks earlier and asked for a meeting in Edinburgh.

So I said OK, let's get it organised. I went to meet him and he asked me what I wanted to do about my future.

I was truthful and I told him I wanted to leave. I let him know that there were a couple of options for me in Italy and possibly even the chance of a move to the English Premiership.

He didn't seem to understand what I was saying. I worry about the chairman you know. Sometimes I think he suffers from selective hearing. Anyway, he said: "Well, what about signing another contract to stay with us?"

I looked at him as if he was crazy. What a stupid suggestion this was. I mean, had he not seen what had happened to me under Advocaat? It was ridiculous.

So I said I would not be signing and to my amazement he asked me why. "OK," I thought to myself, "He's asked for it..."

So I told him straight. There was no holding back. I told him what I thought about Advocaat. I told him what I thought about our dressing room.

But most of all I told him that this club had changed for the worse and that it was no longer the Glasgow Rangers that he owned when I had first signed.

And I said: "Look, you don't need to speak to me to find this out. You don't have to speak to any of the players.

"If you want to know how bad things are then all you have to do is go to Ibrox and speak to the other people who work there every day. Speak to the secretaries, the kit man or even the ladies in the kitchen. Ask them what they think about Advocaat's rules and the atmosphere he has created at Ibrox.

"Then you will understand what I am talking about."

And that's more or less how we left it. He said something about the contract and I said I would think about it.

But I hadn't. Not until now, as I sat watching the tears streaming down Jorg's face. I knew what this club meant to him. He had been here too through the good years and the club had penetrated his heart the same way as it had got into my own.

I think it was suddenly hitting him now. I think he realised he was making a terrible mistake.

I was so sad for him. It is painful even now just thinking about it because Jorg was so happy at Rangers and this was tearing him apart on the inside.

I went back to Italy for five weeks and attempted to sort things out once and for all. There were a lot of meetings with agents and lot of talking had to be done and at the end of it all Lazio and Bologna had emerged as my two real options.

But back home the chairman had not forgotten about me. I know this because he must have phoned me about 10 times that summer and every conversation was exactly the same. "Come on Lorenzo, sign the contract – you know it makes sense."

I tried my best to ignore him and even although I returned to Glasgow to begin the pre-season work with the rest of the team I continued to talk with Lazio.

The manager there was Sven Goran Eriksson. I feel I should point this out because, well, he gets mentioned in all the best books these days doesn't he?

But fate was about to intervene in Lorenzo's life once again as Eriksson was also a wanted man that summer.

In September of 2001 I got a phone call through the night from my agent telling me he had spoken with Lazio and everything had been agreed. The president, Sergio Cragnotti, had promised me a three-and-a-half year contract.

I said: "Fine. Let's get a meeting arranged and get everything finalised."

Eriksson was the guy who wanted me but he was also embroiled in a big row at that time because he had already agreed to become the next manager of England and there was pressure on him to leave Italy immediately to begin his new job.

So two days later my agent phoned again. "Lorenzo, you're not going to believe this. Dino Zoff has been put in charge at Lazio and he doesn't like you. This deal might collapse."

Less than a week later Jaap Stam had signed for Lazio from Manchester United for £15 million. They could have got me for £3 million. But it was their choice and I have to admit that by now Mr Murray was starting to win me over in any case. He had been determined not to let me go all summer.

In fact shortly after I began the pre-season training the chairman decided it was time for another one of our little chats. He said: "Lorenzo, this is a very good offer. Don't throw the money away because this is your future.

"We don't want you to leave. The fans love you, I like you too and I want you to play for this club. You are one of the few who can do a job for this team."

He was being very charming and very persuasive. It was like the summer of 1997 all over again when I signed my first contract with Rangers. Suddenly I started to feel wanted again by Rangers for the first time in a long, long time. I must admit it felt good.

But before anything was agreed I hurt my shoulder and returned to Italy for something like four weeks for more rehabilitation. During that period everything was on hold. Everything except the chairman that is.

He phoned me up again and started pulling my leg. He said: "You see, I told you. If only you had signed that contract everything would be OK. Now look at you. You're injured, you don't have a contract and now who knows what's going to happen?"

I laughed and told him there was no reason for me to panic. I knew I would be back quickly and I knew I would be back to my best. I also knew that we were very close to agreeing something with Lazio but then came the call to inform me that Zoff was not my greatest fan.

So once again I arranged to return to Glasgow. I was starting to feel better and better about going back to Scotland. It felt almost as if I was going home. Of course, I didn't admit it to anyone but secretly I was looking forward to getting back.

I returned at the beginning of October and by the end of that month I had signed a new contract. It was a complete u-turn. The chairman had got me again just like he probably always knew he would. And maybe just like I always hoped he would too.

What no-one knew though, was that Bolonga wanted me as well and I came very close to accepting their offer. The guy who had bought me for Fiorentina from Bari was there now as director of football.

He phoned me and told me not to sign anything with Rangers. He promised me that Bologna would give me a contract in January 2002. All I had to do was sit tight for four months and then I would get my move.

But that was a risk I was not prepared to take. If they had given me something to sign which guaranteed that the deal would be done in January then, yes, I probably would have accepted it.

But they couldn't do that and so I was left with just one offer on the table. I decided I would take it – even if it meant working with Advocaat again.

Now you have to understand here that, even if my heart was still blue, this was not an easy decision to make because I didn't know if I would be able to cope with being one of Advocaat's players again.

I had managed to stay calm throughout all of our problems but probably only because I thought it would only be a matter of time until we parted company for good. Now, though, I was about to commit myself to him for another three years.

The truth is, I was worried I might snap if we had another disagreement and I told the chairman this as well.

What if I lost all control? What if I could not help myself? What if the rage I had been suppressing for so long suddenly all came gushing out and I did something very regrettable indeed? You never know what can happen in this kind of situation.

You can take it and take it and take it but sooner or later you are going to explode.

That is why I would probably have taken the ticket to Bologna had they been able to give me a guarantee. OK, maybe it would have been the easy way out but it seemed like a good idea at the time.

The thing was, though, that all the time there was a nagging voice telling me that I could not make the same mistake as Jorg Albertz.

Besides, I was honestly beginning to feel as if Rangers wanted me again and that was all I had ever really hoped for.

So, for all of these reasons, I ignored my head, gave into my heart and agreed to go back into the trenches beside the man who had tried to plunge a knife into my back.

The day after I signed the contract Advocaat called me over to him on the training ground and, in front of all the assembled photographers, he shook my hand and said: "Congratulations."

I must admit this gesture took me completely by surprise and from that moment we actually started to get closer to each other again.

But he didn't stop there. He spoke to the media and said some very nice things about me. Suddenly everything had changed and I decided I had to make an effort to build bridges with him too. I'm not stupid, I knew what I had to do.

For a long time I had only ever spoken to him about football. We talked when we had to talk - that was it. But now it was time to reach a compromise - we both knew it - and so we started the season hand in hand.

It was an unlikely alliance, maybe even an uneasy alliance, but what I did not know was that this would only be a temporary arrangement.

The season began badly. Hold on, no it didn't - the season began disastrously.

In early August we went out of the Champions League against Fenerbahce. I did not play in the first game against the Turks at Ibrox. In fact we had so many injuries it was almost like a reserve side we had out there that night.

We drew 0-0 but we knew we would get some players back before we travelled to Istanbul and we believed we would finish the job over there.

What followed was quite incredible. Before that game the referee, a countryman of mine and an official I had always respected, Pierluigi Collina, went on what could only be described as a lap of honour around the stadium.

The Turkish fans started chanted his name and he even waved back to them. I had never seen anything like it before and I don't think I ever will again. It was a very bad way for a referee to behave.

He went on to have a shocking game starting in the first couple of minutes when he awarded the free-kick which led to Fenerbahce's opening goal. It was a terrible decision.

I told him to his face that I didn't like what he was doing to us. He said: "If you want to speak to me again do it in English. I don't want people here thinking that we are old friends from Italy."

I shook my head and said: "Oh, just f**k off!". He didn't appreciate my suggestion. He booked me for it.

I have watched a video of that game a few times since and I

still don't understand what Collina was doing that night. There were many strange decisions made, awful decisions, and I will always wonder about Collina's performance because this was so unlike him. Of course, referees can have bad games just like players but I must admit I found this one very upsetting.

Only Collina knows for sure what went on inside his head that night in Turkey. I can only guess. I found it all very suspicious but in my heart I don't really believe that anything sinister went on over there. At least I don't want to believe it because I have always trusted referees and considered them to be honest.

But what I will say is that some of the refereeing in the recent World Cup Finals in Japan and Korea raised a lot of new questions in my mind. In Italy there was a lot of controversy about the way our team went out against Korea but I believe that Spain suffered a far greater injustice when they went out against the same host nation.

I prefer not to think too much about these incidents because they have left a black cloud hanging over this business of mine and I like to believe that the game's officials are not corruptible.

In any case, if you start to doubt the men in the middle then you can sometimes find excuses for your own failings when they simply do not exist.

No, Collina did not help us in Istanbul but we still made enough chances to win that game and we didn't take them so our season got off to the worst possible start.

But it was in Europe that we later salvaged our pride.

At home, however, we were struggling for results again and Celtic were leaving us behind. The title was over by Christmas.

But I could see signs that we were improving and I certainly felt that the spirit and camaraderie among the players was starting to return.

We were certainly playing better football and, apart from the 2-1 defeat away to Fenerbahce, we did not lose any games until the last day of September when we played Celtic for the first time amd went down 2-0 at Ibrox.

Under O'Neill, of course, they had developed a horrible habit of winning these derby games but I should say once again at this point that this had much more to do with us than them.

If you asked me today to walk into Celtic's dressing room and pick anyone I wanted for our team then I would take Henrik Larsson – nobody else. It's not a hard choice to make because he is a wonderful player and a great finisher.

Stilian Petrov is another player that I respect and I might take him with me as well. It would give the Gaffer a great headache if he had to pick between Barry, Mikel, Fernando and Stilian.

There is no question in my mind that we have more talented players than them. They are stronger physically but we know that is a side of our game that we can work on.

There is nothing Celtic's players can do on the training field that will make them as skilful as Mikel Arteta for example.

Another of the players I admire at Parkhead is my old sparring partner Chris Sutton.

In fact, one of the features of the Old Firm matches in the last couple of seasons has been my battles with the Celtic striker. We have had some very fierce tussles and he is, without doubt, one of the most physical players I have come up against – certainly in my time in Scotland.

We have had our disputes on the park. We have both been shown cards by the referees for fouls against each other and we have knocked each other about on occasions. But one thing has never changed and that is my respect for him as a worthy opponent.

Some fans might be surprised by that but just because we don't like each other on the pitch doesn't mean that it should carry on when the final whistle blows.

He plays with determination and passion. So do I. And when we meet we are giving everything to bring success to our teams. That means collisions and confrontations are inevitable. We both want to win but that doesn't mean there has to be hatred.

Don't get me wrong here – Sutton can be nasty on the pitch. But it is his job to unsettle defenders and he does it well. I think he is nasty in a good way for his team and I don't mean he is dirty. He is just very hard. Anyway, many people have said in the past that football is a man's game and you need power and strength as much as the finer points of the game.

Celtic play hard, fast, aggressive football and when they signed Sutton they got someone who fits in with their style. Along with his team-mate John Hartson he is the most physical striker in the Scottish game.

At the end of each game we offer each other our hands and they are shaken. That's how it has got to be. Never forget it is a football game.

I suppose you have to hand it to Celtic because they have worked hard to build a great team spirit and that undoubtedly is what carried them to two successive titles.

But strangely enough it was the steps we made in Europe last season which would lead to us becoming a force to be reckoned with once again in the domestic game.

We started to rediscover ourselves again in the UEFA Cup even if the campaign didn't start too cleverly.

For a long time it looked as if the game's rulers were determined to send us into war-torn Chechnya to play against Anzhi Makhachkala. Eventually, after threatening to withdraw us from the competition, Mr Murray won the battle and UEFA agreed to let us play a one-off tie in Poland.

This was a great gesture from the chairman as we had already cost the club a lot of money by failing to qualify for the Champions League and so, financially, we badly needed a run in the UEFA Cup.

But, after receiving advice from the British Govenrment, he felt our lives would be in danger if we went to Makhachkala and he was not prepared to take that risk - no matter how much money was involved.

So he fought UEFA on our behalf. And he won. I don't believe there are many chairmen in this game of ours with the moral fibre or the strength of character to do such a thing.

So we went to Warsaw where a goal in the last minute from Bert Konterman finally killed off the Russians and set us up for a memorable campaign.

In the next round we took care of Moscow Dynamo, 7-2 on aggregate, and then in December we faced Paris Saint German knowing that if we could get through this round then we would be the first Rangers team in nine years to stay in Europe until after Christmas.

We drew the first game 0-0 at Ibrox and then went to Paris for the second leg where, I have to say, I think I played the game of my life.

We won it on penalties and by the end I was in tears. It meant so much to me.

After all the problems we had experienced we felt we had really achieved something as a team. And personally it was a great feeling for me after everything I had been through.

I remember looking at our fans as they celebrated. There were something like 10,000 of them in the Parc Des Princes that night and it gave me unbelievable joy to see them going wild when it was all over.

These fans had also suffered so many disappointments, especially in Europe, so we felt we had given them something back. This was a memory that we could all cherish.

And perhaps more importantly, our dressing room was finally back together again. Everything was falling back in to place.

After that game Advocaat was very emotional. He came to me and hugged me. He told me I was fantastic. I must admit I got emotional as well. Well, it was a monumental moment in this strange relationship of ours. I had never imagined there could ever be such warmth between us again and yet here we were hugging each other and feeling that, together, we had really achieved something.

It was as if Rangers had suddenly become one big family again the way it always used to be and the way it always must be.

But life is never simple and so even in this fantastic moment our team had to suffer a heavy blow.

Claudio Reyna told us after the game that he was leaving to go to Sunderland. He broke the news to the rest of us on the team bus on the short journey from Glasgow Airport back to Ibrox. He was going straight home to get his bag packed and then travelling down south through the night.

I couldn't believe what he was telling us. I said: "Claudio, what the f**k are you thinking about? Sunderland?"

But his mind was made up. I don't know if it was just because he wanted to play in the Premiership - he didn't say - but I still believe he did it for the same reason as all of the others, because of what had been happening to our team over the previous 18 months.

I couldn't put my hand on my heart and say it for sure but I really think he had simply been sickened by it all. I can't see any other reason for him moving to Sunderland and I know what I'm talking about because, of course, I had once been faced with the same choice.

Had it been Arsenal or Manchester United or even Leeds or

Liverpool then we would have understood. But Sunderland?

I sometimes wonder if Claudio regrets making that move now. I also wonder if he would have changed his decision had he only known about the incredible change that was about to take place at Ibrox just a few days later.

That weekend I played against Hearts, I think we won 3-0, but then I had a suspension to serve which would keep me out of the team for three weeks.

So I asked Advocaat if I could go back to Italy for one week to see my parents at Christmas and he said he didn't have a problem with that. I flew home on the Sunday morning while the rest of my team mates were preparing for a midweek game against Hibs.

On the Tuesday I phoned Laura, the manager's secretary and a very nice lady who I can talk to about anything.

Anyway, we started chatting and then she said: "Lorenzo, we might be getting a new manager."

At first I didn't believe her so I asked what she was talking about. I thought maybe this was some kind of joke.

But she said: "No, seriously, I think Advocaat will be leaving after our game against Hibs and Alex McLeish will be taking over."

I said: "What? The manager of the same Hibs team we are playing against tomorrow? How can that happen?"

What was McLeish supposed to do? Take his team to Ibrox to play against Rangers and then wave them goodbye from the front door when they got back onto the team bus afterwards?

I was very nearly lost for words. Honestly!

As it turned out McLeish was appointed as our new manager before the game but Advocaat took charge of the team for one last time. We could only manage another draw.

Then, when I woke up on the Thursday morning, and before

I had left my house to go training, I got a call on my mobile. I knew it was from Scotland because the number came up on the screen. The conversation went something like this.

"Hello, who's speaking?"

"Hi Lorenzo, it's the manager here."

"Who?"

"It's Alex McLeish here."

"Oh, boss, how are you doing? I hear it wasn't a good result last night?"

"Depends which team you're talking about!"

And straight away I knew I was going to enjoy working with this man. Think about it.

I had played under Advocaat for three-and-a-half years and he hardly ever called me on the phone during all of that time. Now, one day into the job, the new man was calling me up and cracking jokes. I knew that things had suddenly taken a turn for the better. I had a good feeling about this.

But I was also very surprised and maybe even a little bit disappointed in Advocaat for walking away from the job when he knew that we had a massive game still to come against Feyenoord for a place in the quarter-finals of the UEFA Cup.

He had taken us so far - becoming a hero again in the eyes of our supporters - and now he was getting out when our journey was only just starting.

Half of me felt it was as if this was Advocaat saying: "I will go out as the manager who kept Rangers in Europe after Christmas for the first time in nine years."

It was almost as if he had put his own reputation in front of the good of the club.

But then the other half of me thought that maybe the guy is just doing the honest thing here with the good of the team at heart. Maybe he realises his time is up and that if he stays in our dressing room any longer he will only do more harm than good.

If you asked me today then I would have to say it was the latter of the two. I believe he did it for all the right reasons but who knows what went on?

I'm not even sure if he resigned or if he was advised to resign by the chairman. My gut feeling is that they got together to find a compromise and they did it in the best interests of the club.

You might also expect me to say that I was delighted to see the back of him. Funnily enough, you would be wrong. This was not a personal triumph for Lorenzo Amoruso.

But, I have to admit, after speaking to the new man I sensed there would be better times ahead both for myself and for Rangers.

I also felt sorry for Jorg, Claudio and the others and, in fact, one of the first things I did after McLeish had taken over was to go to him and ask if there was any way we could bring Jorg back from Hamburg.

I said: "Listen, I have spoken to Jorg and I don't think he's happy back in Germany. He knows he made a mistake when he left this club. Why don't we try to sign him right away."

It made perfect sense as I was sure Hamburg would be reasonable with their demands. After all, they had an unhappy player in their team and he was one of the highest earners at the club.

Alex said he would think about it and he did. But a week later he came back to me and said: "Lorenzo, I would love to bring Jorg back here but I just don't think we can do it."

The big problem, of course, was Advocaat. Alex couldn't do it because Advocaat was now the club's director of football and the two of them were working together as a team.

If Alex had made Jorg Albertz his first signing then he was sending out the message that Advocaat had got it all wrong.

That was something that he simply could not do.

But I remain certain that, if circumstances had been different, then Alex would have at least tried to bring Jorg back home and I know for a fact that Jorg would have come back because he told me so.

Alex even told me that he loved Jorg as a player so I urged him to give it some more thought. I said: "Look, everybody knows that Advocaat will probably be leaving in one year's time anyway."

But it was just too difficult. Too much water had gone under the bridge and so sadly there would be no place for my old friend on this exciting new adventure.

# *Chapter Twelve*

## SMILES BETTER

MAN-MANAGEMENT is one of the most important weapons in any manager's armoury. If a boss can keep a squad of players happy, particularly a squad with more than a few big egos, he is well on his way to being a success.

Alex McLeish's skills in this department are as good as any I have ever seen in a football manager. And make no mistake – it is his ability to make players want to do well for HIM as well as the club that has contributed to the success he has enjoyed in the year since he replaced Advocaat.

He has shown that a laugh can be more effective than a lash. There is a lot of fun at Murray Park and Ibrox these days and not only the players are smiling. You look around the office staff, the cleaners, everybody. They are happy to be connected with Rangers and this wasn't always the case.

McLeish scored a massive victory with the dressing room less than two weeks after he came to the club.

As we've already established, players at a club like Rangers are well paid and have a lot of privileges but there are also sacrifices to be made. One of those is that we give up the right to enjoy Christmas the way almost everyone else does.

Invariably, we have to play on Boxing Day which means that traditionally as you are all tucking into your turkey, we are in at work preparing for the following day's game. That goes with the territory and so we just get on with it.

Last year's Boxing Day fixture was against Hibs in Edinburgh - a match against the club McLeish had just left and whose fans were very upset about it. It promised to be a very tough game and we all knew that the boss would be desperate to win it for a number of reasons.

On the morning of Christmas Eve he called a meeting of the players and said something that made us all look at each other in astonishment.

He said: "Guys, I know that this is a difficult time of the year to be away from your family, so I'm giving you tomorrow off."

Now remember this was being said to a group of players who had been conditioned to accepting the most ridiculous rules and regulations imaginable imposed by the previous manager up until just two weeks earlier.

We all thought Christmas had come a day early, to be honest.

McLeish went on to to spell out what he demanded from us in return. We were to stay at home on Christmas Day and get as much rest as possible. But we could eat sensibly and we could even have a drink - as long as we did it in moderation, bearing in mind that we had a game the following day.

We were delighted and the most important thing of all was that he was trusting us. He treated us like mature adults, not silly schoolboys who had to be kept in line with a rulebook.

He added: "I want you all to have a great day and when we get together on Boxing Day, I want you to go out and get a win over there."

So we all enjoyed our Christmas Day off like normal people and when we took the field at Easter Road we played beautifully. We beat them 3-0 which says everything about how we felt about this new manager.

The morale in the dressing room was getting better by the day. The training was good, there were jokes in the dressing room and the rules that had strangled our spirit had been relaxed. It wasn't a holiday camp, of course, but nobody wanted it to be. We just wanted to be able to enjoy coming to our place of work.

McLeish changed a lot of little things but he made things a whole lot better by doing so.

For instance, the nonsense about waiting for the manager to sit down and say: "Enjoy your meal," before you could take your first forkful of lunch was ended immediately.

If we wanted to eat at the training ground we could do so but we were no longer all seated at the one huge table. There were times under Advocaat when about 30 guys were all seated together and it didn't make for the most relaxed meal-times.

McLeish ordered smaller tables that seated three or four and the guys could all split up and enjoy their meals more. After training we could leave whenever we wanted which was also different from the previous regime.

The relationship between McLeish and his assistant Andy Watson - who is a great guy - works very well and there is just a feeling of friendliness about the place that wasn't in evidence before they arrived.

His door is always open for players who might be having problems away from the pitch. There is a feeling of togetherness that the players have responded to in a positive manner.

But it isn't all laughs. When we have to work we knuckle down and give it everything we have. If you want respect, you have to give it back. McLeish gave it to us at Christmas and we have respected him ever since.

Even the players who are not involved in the starting 11 every week are quite happy at the club now because they are still made to feel very much part of the squad. With the other manager, if you were not in the team you were the invisible man. You didn't know why you were out of the team but Alex will explain to you the reason for his decision and again, the players respect that kind of openness.

Some people mistake kindness for softness but that is a big error in my opinion. Alex McLeish is a good man but don't think for a minute that he is soft.

We have seen the other side of his nature as well and believe me, it is better to keep making him happy than it is to get on the wrong side of him.

The first time we saw him angry was actually after his very first game in charge.

We were playing Motherwell at Fir Park and although I was suspended he asked me to fly back from Italy in time to come to the game – and it was then that I saw at first hand how much he wanted to be a winner for Rangers.

We only drew the game and he was angry enough about that. But he was particularly annoyed with Fernando Ricksen because he made a couple of bad tackles after he'd already been booked and he could have been sent off. Luckily, he wasn't, but McLeish still had a real go at him in the dressing room. He also criticised Craig Moore for a very bad tackle that could have brought a red card and he was shouting at the entire defence because he thought they had been sloppy in allowing Motherwell back into a game that should have been won.

I went to the dressing room at the end of the game and saw how angry and upset he was. It showed us that he was hard but we also knew he was fair.

The only other time I have ever seen him so angry was at Berwick - although he was probably just as furious in Zizkov this season but I wasn't there to witness that.

But I was there at Berwick all right and to be fair, each and every one of us deserved the roasting he gave us in that little dressing room.

It was just after New Year and we had been playing a lot of football but that was no excuse for the performance we put in against Berwick Rangers in the third round of the Scottish Cup.

We drew 0-0 and we were absolutely terrible. Everyone apart from Stefan Klos, who didn't really have a lot to do, was shocking and the only positive thing from the night was that we left their ground still in the tournament.

That wasn't good enough for the manager and he let us know in no uncertain terms. He was shouting like a crazy man but it was understandable.

Against small teams like Berwick it was the game of their players' lives. For us, it was just another game that we had to get over and done with. We went out with the wrong attitude and we could have lost it.

Our punishment was that we now had a replay and that meant we had to play four games in a week. The manager had no sympathy for us and he basically sent out the same team who had got us into the mess and ordered us to get us out of it.

We won the replay 3-0 but even then it took about an hour before I scored a free-kick to break Berwick's resistence. But when the goal went in we knew it was over and we were through to the next round.

In between these matches we had to travel to Aberdeen for a league game and this was to erupt into one of the most disturbing I have been involved in with Rangers.

There is a bad feeling between the two sets of supporters and I have been told it relates to a very bad tackle made by the Aberdeen player Neil Simpson on Ian Durrant back at the end of the 1980s.

I know the challenge cost Durranty two years of his career and from what I have been told, it may also have robbed him of the opportunity to be a genuine superstar. I didn't see him playing before the injury, of course, but many people I respect in the game have told me that he was absolutely brilliant.

To be fair, the Ian Durrant I saw playing was still a very good footballer but I accept what these people have told me. Anyway, the Rangers fans have never forgiven Aberdeen for that tackle.

On the other side of the coin, I don't think Aberdeen's supporters have ever been able to handle the fact that their current team isn't nearly as good as the one that won the European Cup Winners' Cup and spent a period under Alex Ferguson dominating the Old Firm and winning the league here in Scotland.

I think they are jealous of Rangers, and to a lesser extent Celtic, and when their team meets us there is always poison in the air.

There certainly was that night at Pittodrie and although I did my best to stop a situation getting out of control, I don't really think I succeeded.

It all started so suddenly. Aberdeen won a throw in in front of the little wedge of the stadium where the Rangers fans were sitting. Robbie Winters came over to take it and the next thing it was raining coins.

Why? I don't know. But some Rangers fans that night did not make their club look good.

The Aberdeen fans were very upset at this and they started breaking seats and throwing them at the Rangers fans. It was all going crazy and I just thought: "I have to try to stop this."

I went to the Rangers fans shouting for them to calm down - what is the point of trying to hurt a player who is trying to take a throw in?

I think I was succeeding. The Rangers support was calming down but out of the corner of my eye to the right I saw some movement and when I spun round, a group of Aberdeen fans were on the touchline obviously trying to make their way to the Rangers section.

At that point the referee decided to take us into the dressing room. It was terrible publicity for the Scottish game because the match was being shown live on television all over Britain.

We all got back into the dressing room and one or two of my team-mates told me I was stupid to get involved - they said it was a job for the police and the stewards to stop a riot, not the players.

But I don't agree. I think if the fans see players - people they look up to - asking them to behave then this will have more of an affect than the stewards going in.

After 20 minutes the referee came into the dressing room and told us that we were going back out to play the game but if anything else happened he would be abandoning the match.

Thankfully when we kicked off again the fans had calmed down a little and there was no further trouble. We won the game 1-0 with probably the best goal I've scored for Rangers - a long range shot with my left foot into the top corner.

That match took place in the middle of January but it was a game three weeks later, in the first week of February, that I believe I saw the balance of power in Scottish football starting to swing back towards Rangers.

Celtic were out in front in the league and McLeish had little chance of bridging the gap by the time he arrived. But there were still two domestic trophies up for grabs and we had reached the semi-final of the CIS Cup.

The luck of the draw had paired us with Celtic at Hampden and this was to be Alex McLeish's first Old Firm match.

We had played well under him and were unbeaten but most of the pundits believed that Celtic would be far too strong for us.

They were to be proved wrong and at the end of an incredible 120 minutes I sensed that everyone, particularly our own fans, had begun to believe that the tide was about to turn in our favour.

We prepared well for that match but just before we went out there, McLeish said to us: "Guys, I did not come here for the money or for the fame. I came here because I want to win things. I want to feel this kind of atmosphere - feel it, you can cut it with a knife.

"You should all want this. This is a one-off and we can win it. Run for everything, challenge for everything and if you believe in yourselves we can beat them."

That night, for the first time in about 18 months apart from the 5-1 game we won, we challenged them physically. We could still play our own style of football but for the first time in a long time they were not better than us in the physical side of the game.

Having said that, it nearly went horribly wrong for us in the very first minute. Arthur Numan was short with a pass and John Hartson was onto it quickly. He took it round Stefan Klos but I read the situation and tucked in behind Stefan. Hartson's angle was restrictive and he could only hit a small part of the goal. To be fair to him, he got his shot on target but I stretched out a leg to divert the ball for a corner.

If we had gone behind so early Celtic would have been on a high and we would have been in trouble. It was a real wake-up call though and it showed we had to be alert. I was proud of that interception and we went on to play well in the first half and finally got our reward when Peter Lovenkrands scored just before half-time. That was the first time in ages we had gone 1-0 up on Celtic and we were delighted.

Unfortunately we lost a goal in the second half and the match was heading into extra-time when I suffered a bad injury that almost forced me to come off.

We had forced a corner and I went for the high ball with their keeper Rab Douglas. As we hit the ground together his studs landed on my thigh, boring deep into my flesh.

It wasn't even a normal cut because the studs twisted inside my leg and to this day I still have a strange scar.

It was a very deep cut. I could look inside it and see the muscle moving and throbbing. I think both Neil Lennon and Douglas saw it too and they said it almost made them throw up. The doctor was asking if I could go on and I didn't know because I was lying down.

I was behind the goal at the Rangers end of the ground and when I got to my feet to test my leg, there was this huge roar that seemed to shake the stadium.

It was as if all 25,000 of them were shouting: "You can't go off Lorenzo - we need you."

My leg was sore. In fact it was agonising but I knew there was no tear in the muscle so I could continue. There was no way I was going off - not with those fans urging me on. This was the greatest anaesthetic I could have asked for. Adrenaline took over and saw me through the rest of the match.

I just told the doctor to bandage me up and let me get back

out there. It was crucial that I carried on because earlier in the match my partner Craig Moore had to go off with a hamstring injury and to lose both of us would have been a major blow against a team that was full of tall players who could use their aerial strength to their advantage.

I thought about what McLeish had said in that dressing room and I knew I had a job to do for him and for this team of ours.

So I played on and when the match went into extra-time Bert Konterman became the hero with one of the best strikes you will ever see.

He caught the ball just perfectly from 30 yards and as it ripped into the net we knew Celtic would not come back.

We were all delighted for Bert and no-one more than me because I have suffered from the kind of stick that he has taken in the past so I knew how much scoring that goal meant to him.

I remember hearing the Celtic fans cheering with sarcasm when Bert's name was read out over the speakers before the game. They gave a huge cheer and were trying to be funny.

Well Bert had the last laugh that night and it was great to hear the Rangers fans chant his name long after the final whistle and for the next few weeks.

It was a massive result for us. In a country where two teams dominate the rest you cannot afford to lose to your great rival and for us, losing to Celtic was becoming a bad habit.

But we had broken it and to do so in Alex McLeish's first game against them was very significant.

It gave us belief and I think it helped Alex become accepted by our supporters. Some of them had questioned the wisdom of the appointment in December because they wanted a more experienced man or a bigger name. But none of those voices were to be heard that night or after it.

We now believe we are as good as Celtic whereas in the past, I have looked around our dressing room before Old Firm matches and wondered if some of the players really believed they could win. That has now changed.

You just have to look into the eyes of the players in the dressing room and in the tunnel before these games. Like the Rocky movie, we have the eye of the tiger...we are determined not to be beaten by them.

For Alex to remain unbeaten against our oldest rivals in his first season as manager was hugely important and gave us back our self belief.

The semi-final victory led to another big Hampden occasion in the Final against Ayr United, a First Division club who had done brilliantly to get so far in the competition.

Our fans thought we only had to turn up to lift the trophy but this was Ayr's big day and their players were always going to give it everything.

To their credit they played great football in the first half and gave us a few problems. We had Stefan to thank for a couple of fine saves to keep them out. Then just before half time, Tore Andre Flo scored from a very difficult chance to give us the lead and break the hearts of our brave opponents.

If we thought we'd get a pat on the back from the boss at the interval we were wrong. He went through us and called the performance a joke. He questioned our desire and he demanded much more after the break.

He was right of course, and his words had the desired effect. We concentrated harder, made fewer mistakes and were more ruthless up front. We ran out 4-0 winners and at last we had a trophy in our hands.

It was a great moment for Barry Ferguson - the first time he had lifted a trophy as captain. I knew what that feeling was like and of course it was in my mind that if Advocaat had not taken the armband from me I would have been going up those stairs first.

While I was standing on the pitch at the end of the game I made the conscious decision that if I could not be first up to collect the CIS Cup, I would be the last.

It was a great feeling to lift the trophy, no matter where I was in the line-up, and the Rangers fans gave me a huge cheer as I raised the silverware to the sky before we all ran onto the pitch to do our lap of honour.

While we celebrated that day I couldn't help think back to about three weeks earlier when we threw away the opportunity to record a much more significant victory.

After beating PSG in the UEFA Cup we had been drawn against another top European side, Feyenoord, in the fourth round. It was a tough draw but one that gave us a 50/50 chance of going through.

With so many Dutchmen in our team and with Feyenoord having the former Celtic striker Pierre van Hooijdonk in their ranks, there was no shortage of hype going into the first match at Ibrox.

To be honest, we didn't perform anywhere near our capabilities and couldn't complain when they took the lead through their Japanese player Ono.

However we kept battling away and finally drew level through a penalty from Barry so we travelled to Rotterdam still believing we had a chance of making the quarter-finals of the competition.

On the night the real Rangers turned up and we played Feyenoord off the park and still lost. It was heartbreaking.

We scored early but near the interval, van Hooijdonk started falling about as soon as anyone looked at him and conned the referee into giving free-kicks within range of the goal.

There is more to Pierre's game than that, which is a good

thing, because there is nothing in the game that annoys me more than divers.

I hate seeing players fall over as if they've been shot when you merely brush them, or even when you don't touch them at all.

Diving is a terrible part of our sport and although it is becoming more commonplace in Scotland, I still don't think it is nearly bad as it is in Italy and I hope it never catches up.

I can't understand why referees let players away with it. It is cheating - nothing more or less - and those who do it should be punished but almost always they get away with it.

Winning games this way is nothing to be proud of in my opinion. There are some players who are serial divers. They do it again and again and get away with it. In Italy, two of the worst offenders are Filippo Inzaghi of Juventus and Marco Delvecchio of Roma. But in Scotland I don't see it as much. The footballing culture here is more of hard work and honesty on the park and that should be applauded. It does happen sometimes of course, but I don't think there is one player here who everyone knows will be diving in every game.

But the Italians and Spanish are bad for it. As for the Germans - they are the world champions at it. They've learned well from the Italians.

When we played against Bayern Munich in the Champions League three years ago it was the worst I have ever seen. They dived for 90 minutes - all of them - and they scored an equaliser from a free-kick that came from a dive in injury time. It was one of the most frustrating nights of my career.

One dive did cause me to smile a few days after it happened though, and I promise you it was not because it led to a Celtic defeat.

In a Champions League game in Turin last season, Celtic lost 3-2 to Juventus because of a last minute penalty when Nicola Amoruso, who is no relation, appeared to dive inside the box as

Joos Valgaeren challenged him.

The following Saturday we were playing in a match when suddenly the Rangers fans starting singing: "There's Only Two Amorusos." I couldn't stop laughing and neither could my team-mates.

We were not laughing at Celtic's misfortune but we found the humour of our supporters very funny that day.

Anyway, that night in Rotterdam we were made to pay a heavy price for van Hooijdonk's theatrics. He is not just an actor - he is a dead ball specialist and in my opinion one of the best in Europe - and he displayed all his quality that night.

He scored with two free-kicks, although we didn't cover ourselves in glory defending them and from being in control, we were suddenly up against it.

Worse was to follow when we went 3-1 down but at that point we rallied and they had a man sent off for a foul on Michael Mols inside the box. Barry scored from the spot and now it was 3-2 and they were a man down.

We pounded them but the goal wouldn't come. Claudio Caniggia missed a chance, Michael had an opportunity as did Peter Lovenkrands but we couldn't break through and when Neil McCann showed dissent after being denied a clear foul, he was sent off and with the numbers evened up, Feyenoord held out.

But they knew and we knew that the better team was out of the competition and they rubbed salt into the wound by going all the way and winning the UEFA Cup.

I'm not saying we would have done likewise because you just never know what will happen in football. But I believe we had a real chance and if it had not been for those two free-kicks, we might just have written our names in the pages of this club's history last season.

When you have a trophy in your hands, it doesn't matter who you've beaten to win it. But for Rangers fans it is always sweeter when the team going up to get the runners-up medals is Celtic.

That's the treat we gave them on Saturday, May 4 and hopefully it made up for the disappointment of seeing our rivals win the championship a week or two earlier.

The two league games between us since the CIS Cup Final had been drawn and we had played well in both - particularly at Parkhead - but most experts were predicting that Celtic, after their title success, would go on to complete the double.

We weren't bothered about that because we knew what we had to do. But our plans were almost blown out of the water by an accident that happened to me on the day before the cup final.

We were training when I suddenly felt a big problem in my back. We were practising set-pieces when my back suddenly locked. I couldn't move and I was in a great deal of pain.

My first reaction was: "I've no chance of playing tomorrow,"and I was devastated because I had also missed our last Scottish Cup Final against Aberdeen through injury.

The medical staff weren't about to give up hope though and they contacted a chiropractor who would come to Murray Park in the early evening before the final.

I waited for him while the team boarded the bus that would take them to the Moat House Hotel where we were staying on the Friday night. At that point I still didn't think I would be joining them later.

The chiropractor manipulated my back and gave me an injection for the pain. He then told me that if I felt any better in the morning I could play in the game but warned that I would be nowhere near 100 percent fit. The muscles were inflamed and I would not be able to move fluidly.

I turned up at the hotel and went to bed shortly afterwards.

But I couldn't sleep properly because I was worried about how I would feel the next day and whether I would be able to play.

Eventually, I drifted off to sleep but it seemed like I was dreaming for only two minutes when an alarm started going off in my head. I thought: "It can't be time to get up already," then I realised that it was the hotel fire alarm that was ringing loudly in my ears.

I got gingerly out of bed and made my way downstairs with the rest of my team-mates and other hotel guests. It was four o'clock in the morning of the biggest game of the season and we were standing outside in the cold by the River Clyde for half-an-hour while firemen went through the motions of checking for a fire that we knew didn't exist.

Someone set that alarm off knowing that Rangers were staying there that night. It was a hoax but there were a lot of Celtic fans in the hotel that evening and there's no doubt in my mind that they did it to try to disturb our night's sleep.

We were all absolutely furious - but the calmest man was Alex McLeish. He knew it was a false alarm but he told us to take it in our stride. When he had been playing for Aberdeen against the Old Firm the same thing had happened regularly to him. He just laughed and said it wouldn't stop us winning the game. And you know what? That episode made us all the more determined to beat Celtic that afternoon. As we stood there in the cold and the dark we spoke about it. And I was more determined than ever that I would play my part.

We were eventually allowed back to our beds and when I finally woke up the next morning it was with great relief that I felt my back and discovered that it was a lot better than it had been.

It still was nowhere near perfect, however, but if the manager thought I could do a job for him at 65-70 per cent of my full fitness then I was willing to give it a go.

I could jump and head the ball when it was coming straight towards me but when it was coming in from wide areas and I was having to twist, I was having big problems.

I knew it would be a tough afternoon because Celtic have so many big strong men and they like to throw balls into the box and fight for them in the air. They've got guys like Hartson, Sutton, Balde and Mjallby who can take advantage of that tactic and you have to be able to compete with them for the high balls.

We knew they could cause us problems from set-pieces or long balls so all I was thinking about was keeping things simple. If the ball was there to be won, forget the pain, attack it and get it away.

But we lost two goals and both were from set-pieces. Balde got up and headed one down for Hartson to score and the second one came from a cross from a wide area when I couldn't jump properly because of my back and Balde scored. I was very upset because I knew if I had been fully fit I could have made a better challenge.

In between those goals, Peter Lovenkrands had scored with a great shot to make it 1-1 but when Balde put Celtic 2-1 ahead we were in trouble.

That's when the character of the team shone through. We had been the better team throughout the match but we were behind with only about 12 minutes to go. Barry had been superb all through the game and when I won a free-kick on the edge of the Celtic box - Balde had pushed me as I tried to flick a ball into the penalty area - he curled a brilliant free kick into the corner of the net.

We exploded with delight and relief and at that moment I felt sure the cup was destined to come to Ibrox. Celtic were more tired than us and the pyschological blow of losing the goal when they had one hand on the trophy was massive.

Having said that, I thought we'd have to wait until extra-time to seal the victory - but thankfully Peter made sure that didn't happen.

Peter has electrifying pace and he has the great gift of being able to turn on a performance when it is most needed and as the match moved into injury-time he spotted Neil McCann shaping to cross into the box and timed his arrival perfectly.

A nod of the head and the ball was nestling in the corner of the net. There was no time for Celtic to respond and as we ran to our fans we knew we had won the Scottish Cup.

It was a wonderful end to the season but it didn't take long for us to start thinking about this current campaign. Winning two cups was great but the fact remained that the championship trophy was sitting at Celtic Park.

We want it back and we have started this season in the correct manner. Well, if you remove the UEFA Cup from your memory banks we have.

I can't believe we are out of Europe. Last season we made people sit up and take notice of the name Glasgow Rangers. This time round we have gone out to a team that should have been disposed of without any problem.

I had never even heard of Viktoria Zizkov, from the Czech Republic, but when we were drawn against them I was happy enough because I was confident we'd go through no problem.

I got injured a couple of weeks before the first leg and was allowed to go home to see my parents from a while, so I was in Italy when the first-leg was being played in Prague.

When I turned on the teletext to see the score I could not believe my eyes. Zizkov 2 Rangers 0. How the hell could that be right?

Apparently everyone back in Scotland was saying the same and when I got back the boys admitted they hadn't played at all well.

The boss was furious, of course, but we felt they weren't a great team and at Ibrox we should still overturn the deficit.

The return leg was just incredible. We got the two goals back in the 90 minutes through Ronald de Boer and just into extra time Neil McCann put us three up and that should have been us through.

But a few minutes later, we lost a freak goal - the ball spun up crazily after a challenge by Kevin Muscat and fell to one of their players who scored.

We threw everything at them after that and I was convinced we would score. But someone upstairs was on the goalkeeper's side that night. He made a save from me that I still can't believe and that I haven't been able to bring myself to watch on the video.

The referee gave us a penalty then changed his mind. Stefan Klos came up for a corner and watched the other keeper save his header. It was madness but when the final whistle sounded, Rangers were out of Europe.

McLeish didn't rant and rave in the dressing room. He said what we already knew - that we lost the tie in the first leg. One thing for certain - everyone at Ibrox, from the manager downwards, took this tie seriously. But the fact is we lost to a team we should have beaten and it hurt us badly.

So now we have only the domestic trophies to attack and at the time of writing we are top of the league, just in front of Celtic. Considering they won the title so easily last season, it is an encouraging start but we know there can be no let up.

It's good to be top but we have done nothing yet - if we are still there in May then we can be happy.

I must admit I am confident. I think we are playing better football than at any time since I came to Glasgow. We don't have a top striker like Larsson, who will score us 30 or 40 goals a season. Ronald has been banging them in for us and has started the season very well but the strength of our team is that we do not rely on only one man to score our goals.

Everybody has been chipping in and we carry a threat throughout the team. We are creating chance after chance and we have the players to take them. Some of the football has been a joy to be a part of.

We are giving teams real problems because they don't know who they should be marking to keep off the scoresheet. If we had one guy who was the main striker, the other team could do everything to keep him quiet and shut off the supply of goals.

But we are killing teams with our passing and movement. Our players are popping up all over the place and a lot of our moves are ending with the goalkeeper picking the ball out of the back of his net. Long may it continue.

# Chapter Thirteen

## THE END?

YOU should have seen Bari 20 or 30 years ago when I was growing up. It was a very scary place.

So, yes, I am proud of myself when I think back to where I came from and compare it with where I am today. I have made a success of myself and I feel no shame in admitting it.

That's why I really mean it when I tell you that being voted Player of the Year by my fellow professionals and being given the captain's armband were so important moments in my life. I'm not saying that just to pay lip service to others or because I feel I am obliged to repay the compliment.

No, believe me, it comes from the heart.

Just think about it for a minute and put yourself in my shoes. I have come to Scotland from Italy and, with all respect, the British people are quite a conservative lot. The last thing you want is to see foreigners coming in and taking over positions of power. For you, British will always be best and that's a sentiment I admire because there is nothing wrong with national pride. It's a good quality.

But it also means that anyone coming in from the outside faces an uphill battle to be accepted and hopefully to prove himself worthy of the invitation.

That being the case, it is difficult enough for any player to come to Britain and enjoy real success. Not only have I won trophies and awards in this country of yours but I was also given the great honour of captaining Glasgow Rangers - the first Catholic captain of this great institution.

I make no apologies for saying these are achievements of which I am rightly very, very proud. Nobody can take these memories and medals away from me. I have written my name in the history books.

That may sound arrogant or a bit big-headed but just think about the number of players who moved to clubs in a different country and have not been able to adjust or make much of an impact at all. I'm not just talking about ordinary players - I'm talking about some great names as well like Ian Rush, Dennis Bergkamp and Thierry Henry who were not as successful as they should have been in Italy. There are actually too many examples to mention.

In fact I look upon it as a personal triumph that I am still here almost six years after arriving from Florence. Very few foreign players last that long so I have every right to feel good about myself.

But that doesn't mean I think my job here is done – far from it. Until the day Rangers say they no longer need me then I will be here, fighting for my place and fighting to keep this club where it belongs, at the very top of Scottish football.

And that's why I also look back with some relief now at the times I came so close to being sold off by Advocaat.

And you know the funny thing? A month or so ago my phone rang and it was Advocaat on the other end of the line. Now, in almost four years together as manager and player, he maybe called me once or twice.

So you can imagine my surprise when I heard his voice especially as just a couple of days earlier he had done an article with the Daily Record in which he talked about our relationship.

But I believe he had been told to phone me by the chairman and by Alex McLeish because they knew I was not happy with his side of the story.

He said he didn't mean to say anything which would upset me and that everything he had said had been for the good of the club and the team. Then he said: "After all, everything has worked out well for you ever since I took that armband away."

"Excuse me?" I said, "What exactly are you trying to say - that I played s**t for two years when we won the Treble and the Double?"

But by the end of the conversation we made our peace.

The way I see it - and this is what I told him - is that what he did and what I did was all done to make the club better. OK, we never did see eye-to-eye and we had a lot of stormy times together. At times it seemed very personal.

But I like to think now that this was never really about Lorenzo Amoruso and Dick Advocaat. It was much bigger than that. It was all about Glasgow Rangers. We are both passionate men and we both gave our heart to this club.

Three years ago I could have killed him but I have no regrets

241

now. I could have slaughtered him in the newspapers, I could have stormed out of Ibrox, I could have accepted that transfer to Sunderland or even the later invitations from West Ham and Lazio.

But if I could go back in time to the summer of 2000, and go through the whole experience again, then I would not do a single thing differently.

Everybody makes mistakes in life. The trick is to learn from those mistakes and take something positive from them all.

It is only a fool who continues to fall into the same traps time and time again. If you learn nothing from the bad times then it will only get worse until your entire life becomes one big nightmare.

I know I have made more than my fair share of mistakes. I've made too many to mention and they haven't all been on a football pitch. But I have learned from each and every one of them and they have made me the player and the man I am today.

This incredible adventure which started way back in 1997 when I arrived in Scotland for the first time has been the greatest experience I could ever have asked for. Everyone back home in Italy thought I was crazy at the time and maybe they had a point because I was comfortable in Florence and I had another four years left on my contract.

But I followed my instincts and now, nearly six years on, I can look back and say with complete certainty that I did the right thing.

I will go home one day and when I do I will return with a head full of memories - some bitter, some happy but all of them will live vividly with me until my dying day.

I still have one-and-a-half years to go on my contract. When that deal is over I will be 33-years-old and I will have been in Scotland for seven years. Three more years and I'll qualify for a testimonial - actually, come to think of it, that's not a bad idea.

But seriously, I don't know what the future will hold for Lorenzo Amoruso. If I have learned anything from my time here it must surely be not to plan any further than beyond the end of the next day.

But what would I like to happen? Now that's a different question entirely and it's one that I can answer without the need for any great thought. If the chairman or the manager came to me today and asked me to extend my contract then I would do so, probably without any hesitation.

In a perfect world I would sign a new deal which would see me remaining as a Rangers player until I turn 35 and then, when it is time to go, I will return to Italy and maybe play for enjoyment at a lower level.

Actually, I don't know if I could ever really play just for enjoyment and to keep fit. I want to win things too much just to sit back and play only for fun. It's just part of my nature - even when I play golf or whatever I don't like to finish second.

But when I do call an end to my playing career I know two things. I will return to Italy and I will take one year out from football. It has been my life for as long as I can remember and when I reach 35 I will be ready for a break from it. I will need that time to adjust mentally to the fact that I will be no longer be a football player.

But it won't be a permanent divorce because I think I have something to offer the game in some capacity, be it managing or coaching. That will require a different mentality from that of a player and that is another reason why I will stay away from the game for a year.

I couldn't be a player on the Saturday and then a manager on the Monday. It would be too difficult to make a jump like that. I will have to stand back from it a bit.

One idea that I have been thinking about if I don't go into the coaching or management side of the game is the role of a worldwide scout.

I would love to do that job for Rangers, if they wanted me, of course. I know a lot of football people in Europe and I speak fluently in English and Spanish as well as my native Italian tongue. I love travelling and if I could go around the world looking for and identifying talent I think I could be good at that.

If I could do it for Rangers and that allowed me to continue my association with the club I have grown to love over the past five-and-a-half years I would be honoured and delighted.

That is not a decision I can make, of course, it would be up to Rangers. But what I can say with certainty is that I will be based in Italy – that's for sure. I love Scotland but I have been away from my family and friends for a long time now - it's incredible to think I have spent almost one-fifth of my whole life in Scotland  - and I think when I stop playing for Rangers I will go straight back to my homeland.

I have to make up for lost time with my parents. They are getting older now and I miss them. I need to be closer to them as they head into their old age.

For now, though, I don't plan on going anywhere and I would like to make it clear also that, even if I do end up joining another club when Rangers no longer need me, there will only ever be room for one club in my heart. Believe me.

And whatever I chose to do with my life, when this great adventure is over, you can also be sure that I will do everything I can to be a success.

If I have problems in achieving my goals I will never give up. Never. Life is so strange. One day you can be down and the next day something happens that makes it better. But if you have given up then by the time the good day comes it will be too late.

The reason I say that is this. My first words in this book recorded the events of October 30, 2000. The day Dick Advocaat tried to rip my heart out.

By coincidence, the last of these words is being written today...October 30, 2002.

If I had given up exactly two years ago today I would not have had the satisfaction of beating those who tried to grind me into the dirt.

I did not wave the white flag. I never will.

David McCarthy is a sports writer with The Daily Record. He co-wrote The Martin O'Neill Story last year. He is married to Caroline and lives in Glasgow.

Keith Jackson is the Daily Record's chief football writer and is also a television and radio football analyst. He and his wife Leandra live in Newton Mearns with their beautiful daughter Tyla.